pet rescue

by
Mark Evans
foreword by
Wendy Turner

FOURTH ESTATE • *London*

To Finlay

First published in Great Britain in 1997 by
Fourth Estate Limited
6 Salem Road
London W2 4BU

Text copyright 1997 by Mark Evans
Foreword copyright © 1997 by Wendy Turner

10 9 8 7 6 5 4 3 2 1

A catalogue record for this book is available from the British Library.
ISBN 1-85702-733-7

Photographs on pages 24, 34, 87, 116 and 120 reproduced by courtesy of
the RSPCA
All other photography by Jerry Young
Text design by Planet X
Page make-up by JMP Ltd

Printed in Great Britain by Butler & Tanner, London and Frome

Registered charity no. 219099

The RSPCA receives a two per cent royalty for the sale of every copy of
this book.

Contents

Foreword by
Wendy Turner

PEOPLE OFTEN ASK ME if I cry when faced with some of the cruelty cases we deal with whilst filming for *Pet Rescue*. The answer is always 'No', and the person who has asked the question is often surprised that a vegan and passionate animal lover is not constantly reduced to tears by such close contact with animals that are suffering. The plain facts are that tears don't help the animals (only care, commitment and positive action can do that), and my involvement with animal rights over the years has taught me all too well not to be surprised at the high level of cruelty that the human race can inflict upon the creatures it shares the planet with. It has to be said that many of the cruelty cases I've seen at the RSPCA appear to be the result of complete ignorance rather than malicious intent, although this is hardly of any comfort to the animal that is suffering. Education, however, can deal with ignorance, and I sincerely hope that *Pet Rescue* has gone some way towards making people aware of the massive commitment required when choosing an animal to be a companion.

Some of our stories have sad endings, but many have happy ones. The vast majority of people are acutely aware that the unconditional love given by an animal is something not to be abused, but to be treasured. Animals must have rights and respect and a decent shot at a happy life. Those that get this are indeed the lucky ones, for there's a miserable existence awaiting those that are not so fortunate. For these animals, organisations such as the RSPCA become a lifeline. They offer care and comfort and a fighting chance to make a fresh start. And thank goodness for those people who take on rescued animals and do all they can to give them the lives that they deserve.

Looking after any animal is a huge responsibility, but the rewards are immense. After my parents' dog, Toby, chewed the bottom of the settee, my Dad reasoned that it wasn't worth getting cross over, as not one day had gone by when Toby had not given them cause to smile. Now, how many things in life can you say that about?

Introduction by
Mark Evans

FOR PETS, JUST BEING LOVED ISN'T ENOUGH. If it were, rescue centres around Britain would be near empty, but they're not. Most of them are at bursting point, and many have a waiting list. As soon as a kennel, a cattery place or a rabbit enclosure is vacated, someone else is moved in. Some animals 'in care' are there for very genuine reasons – for instance, they may be victims of abuse or their loving, responsible owners may have died or become too seriously ill to care for them any more. But that's not the story in the majority of cases.

If you're an avid viewer of *Pet Rescue*, by now you'll be only too aware that most rescue-centre residents have been badly let down by people who have failed to take their responsibilities as owners seriously enough. Some of these animals have been neglected because their owners couldn't be bothered to learn how to look after them. Some have wandered off and become strays, and because they were not wearing any form of identification, when found they couldn't be returned home. Some are labelled by their owners as 'problem pets' that are 'off the rails'. In reality, many of them are perfectly normal animals who for one reason or another have found it difficult to adjust to the kind of lifestyle that they have been expected to lead and have not been given the help or guidance they have needed to cope. Other unwanted pets are the result of unplanned pregnancies that could so easily have been prevented. The list goes on. Most, if not all, were loved. Few were cared for properly.

But the past is the past. Nothing can change history. For rescued animals, it is the future that is important.

I take my hat off to those who work in animal rescue, as it's an enormous responsibility. Finding permanent new homes for abandoned and unwanted animals is a tough job made more difficult by the fact that so many would-be animal owners consider those in care to be the second-class citizens of the animal world. They are not, and it seems that *Pet Rescue* is helping to dispel many of the myths and misconceptions that surround animal rescue. I can't tell you the number of people who have come up to me and said that as a result of watching the programme they have decided that when the time is right for them to take on a new animal they will adopt rather than buy.

Initially, our daily appeals were considered by some to be a bit of a gimmick, but viewers have proved those cynics wrong. Over the four months that the programme has been on air, literally thousands of people have called our hotline to offer homes for the animals we have featured, and as a result not only have these animals been found good new owners, but also hundreds more animals have been adopted. Rescue centres all over the country are reporting increased numbers of people through their doors, and it would appear that adoptions are at an all-time high.

But let's not get complacent. It would be so much better for all concerned if animals didn't need rescuing in the first place. Five years at vet school taught me a lot about animals. Ten years as a vet has taught me a whole lot more about their owners. There are good owners and there are bad. Those who think they're good often aren't quite as good as they think they are. The worst have no idea just how bad they are. The very best animal owners are in my experience a rare breed, but they do exist and they're often the most unlikely people. You might expect them all to be breeders, vets, RSPCA inspectors and the like. Of course many of them are, but in my experience most are just ordinary people who both love and respect their animals. These people understand what a privilege it is to live with another kind of animal and never take them for granted. They accept the limits of their knowledge and are always keen to learn more. They constantly question the way they care for their animals and the kind of lifestyle they offer them and dare to be different when other owners simply toe the traditional line. The rewards are huge for both them and the animals they share their lives with.

This book contains many of the most memorable stories from the first series of *Pet Rescue*, together with what I hope you will find to be useful extra information about the pet care and animal welfare issues that they raise. When you read them, feel free to judge the actions of others, but also think hard about why particular problems may have arisen, what the possible solutions might be and what could have been done to prevent the animals from suffering. Take the time to reflect a little on how you yourself treat other animals and how your actions may affect their lives. Think about the animals you live with as well as the many others, such as wild animals and farm stock, whose welfare may partly depend on you. So many animals deserve a better deal than they get. We owe them so much, yet they ask for so little.

Chocolate Chip: a star is born

CHOCOLATE CHIP IS AN EXTRAORDINARY NAME FOR AN EXTRAORDINARY CAT. THEY SAY THAT CATS HAVE NINE LIVES AND I HAVE TO SAY THAT AS A VET, I NEVER CEASE TO BE AMAZED BY THE WAY SOME OF MY FELINE FRIENDS COPE WITH ADVERSITY — NOT JUST ONCE, BUT MANY TIMES OVER. BUT I HAVE NEVER MET A TINY KITTEN WITH SO MUCH FIGHT AS CHOCOLATE CHIP. HE AND HIS NEW OWNER AND LONG-STANDING NURSEMAID, MANDY, ARE A REMARKABLE COUPLE AND A WONDERFUL EXAMPLE OF HOW SPECIAL THE BOND BETWEEN A CAT AND A PERSON CAN BE.

Chocolate Chip was thought to be just a few days old when he was brought into the RSPCA Millbrook Centre in Chobham. The tiny kitten was found by the Graves family, apparently abandoned under a plum tree in their garden. Clifford Graves had heard miaowing for a couple of hours, but as there are many cats in their neighbourhood, he didn't take any notice at first. When the kitten's cries persisted, Clifford and his mother Phyllis went to investigate. Phyllis says, 'I'd never seen such a small cat in all my life!' The little bundle was quickly taken to the RSPCA, where his dark-brown coat inspired staff to name him Chocolate Chip.

Mandy, who is in charge of the cattery at Millbrook, says: 'I couldn't believe he had been brought in without a mum. His eyes weren't even open: kittens' eyelids usually open between three and fifteen days after birth, so we guessed he was about four days old.' Mandy took Chocolate Chip down to the cattery and syringe-fed him a special cat-milk replacement, but she knew it would be much better for him if she could find a new mother who she could try to foster him with.

A few days prior to Chocolate Chip's arrival, Inspector Liz Wheeler had received a call from a woman in Surrey who was concerned that her cat, Duchess, was rejecting her kittens – she wanted the RSPCA to come and collect them. When Liz arrived at the house it wasn't difficult to see why. Duchess and her kittens were on the lino in the middle of a busy kitchen with children running around. The kittens were cold and hungry and the mother was in distress because she didn't have anywhere warm and quiet to look after them. Liz says, 'I picked up one of the kittens, who was soaking wet and like a little ice cube. The mother hadn't even cleaned it up after the birth.'

While the owner was signing the forms for the cats to be rehomed, Liz put the kittens down her bra to keep them warm. As an RSPCA inspector, it pays to be able to think laterally! When she returned to the centre with the cats, it was even more obvious why the mother was in such distress: she hadn't finished giving birth, and an hour later, another kitten was born. After two weeks' recuperation at RSPCA Millbrook, she was given Chocolate Chip to foster, bringing her litter up to four.

Although all cats are vaccinated against 'cat flu' on arrival at RSPCA centres, tragically, Duchess became sick two days later with flu-like symptoms. 'She was a good mum,' says Mandy, 'but she simply didn't have the strength to feed and care for her kittens.' The kittens were taken away to be hand-reared. Duchess rejected all food and couldn't swallow even the liquid meals that the staff prepared for her. She was fighting for her life. Despite all attempts by the staff and the vet to treat and care for Duchess, she died the next day, along with one of her own kittens who had previously not shown any symptoms but deteriorated rapidly.

Devoted friends Chocolate Chip and Mandy together in the stables at RSPCA Millbrook. Like any young cat, Chocolate Chip loves playing games

Meanwhile, staff were lovingly bottle-feeding the other kittens with two-hourly feeds of powdered milk supplement. In the evenings Mandy took Chocolate Chip home with her where he got on very well with her other cats – Pepper, a six-year-old ginger-and-white male, Candy, an eight-year-old black-and-white female, and Bella, a four-year-old tortoise-and-white female that Mandy had rescued from Millbrook. Another Millbrook worker, Sandy, would take home the two surviving kittens from Duchess's litter. All of them responded well. Mandy was able to move Chocolate Chip onto four-hourly feeds and weaned him onto solid food at four weeks. But caring for a kitten is not just a question of feeding. Mandy said she had to 'toilet Chocolate Chip with a piece of wet cotton wool on his bottom'. This may sound distasteful, but it's an essential part of hand-rearing a kitten. If Chocolate Chip had had a mother, she would have done this by licking beneath his tail to stimulate urination and defecation, and then would have eaten what he produced.

Mandy was becoming very attached to Chocolate Chip but suddenly noticed that he was not quite right. He was a little lethargic and not as keen as usual on his food. Then his nose began to run and Mandy knew immediately that he was showing symptoms that could be the same condition that killed his foster mum. She quickly whisked him off to the vet, who took swabs in an attempt to find out exactly what was wrong.

With dedicated nursing, Chocolate Chip improved over the next few days. The swab results proved that he had picked up one of the cat flu viruses and everyone was amazed that the kitten was doing so well. This condition is often extremely serious, and sometimes fatal, in youngsters. But two days later, Mandy's hopes were dashed. On a Saturday evening at home, she noticed that Chocolate Chip's symptoms were returning. He kept moving around in distress and his eyes were very cloudy. She says: 'I was so upset, I rushed him to Sue Walters, the deputy manager at Millbrook, crying my eyes out. My mum had to come with me because she didn't want me driving in such a state.'

Sue cared for Chocolate Chip over the weekend and took him back to the vet first thing on Monday morning. Poor Chocolate Chip – so many things had happened to him in his short life. Mandy was extremely anxious about him and spent the weekend on tenterhooks. This time, she feared that at best Chocolate Chip would go blind because of the cloudiness in his eyes, and at worst that the vet might have to put him down to prevent him suffering further.

But Chocolate Chip was given further treatment and, miraculously, the little fighter bounced back yet again. When Chocolate Chip returned to Millbrook from the vet, Mandy was overcome: she had been terrified that she would never see him again. 'I've been working here for four and a half years with dogs and cats, but I've never been as attached to an animal as I am to Chocolate Chip,' she says.

As Chocolate Chip's health returned, Mandy realised that she would have to think about rehoming him. She had to steel herself to say goodbye to the cat she had grown so inordinately fond of. He would miss her, too. 'The way he looks at me, he knows I'm his mum,' she says. The Graves family, who originally found him under their plum tree, also wanted to adopt him. But, at the eleventh hour, the Graveses relented and Mandy had a reprieve. They could see how close Mandy and Chocolate Chip had become and considered it best for all concerned, especially for Chocolate Chip, that he stayed with her. He'd already had enough disruption in his young life and now he needed stability – another change could retard his development.

Mandy was thrilled with the outcome and took him back to her home where he met up again with her three cats and Desmo, her ten-year-old collie-cross labrador. A playful, mischievous kitten with marked Burmese features, Chocolate Chip is described by Mandy as 'a really happy cat. He's got a brilliant character and is absolutely wonderful. We're completely devoted to each other. He follows me around everywhere and at night when I'm watching TV, he curls up on my lap and goes to sleep. Then, when I go to bed, he sleeps by my bedside. I let him play outside when I'm home, but other than that I keep him in.'

Chocolate Chip is now happy and healthy and thriving in his new home. When he was six months old Mandy had him neutered, in my view a responsible and integral part of cat ownership for those who do not intend to breed from their cats. Every year there are thousands of unplanned cat pregnancies, and many queens (adult female cats) and kittens suffer unnecessarily... a fact that, in her job, Mandy is only too acutely aware of.

Since Chocolate Chip's saga was broadcast on *Pet Rescue* in spring 1997, Mandy has been approached by people in the street who all ask about Chocolate Chip's progress. 'It doesn't bother me at all,' says Mandy, 'it just means that people really care about animals and want to know how he's getting on.' Mandy and Chocolate Chip have been through so much together: 'I wouldn't be able to let him go for anybody – he's mine now.' Mandy has been devoted to all animals and especially cats since she was an infant. 'I've always loved animals, ever since I could walk, and got my first cat at the age of seven. I'll spend the rest of my life caring for animals.'

Could you look after a cat?

Before choosing a kitten there are many things to bear in mind. You must be sure that you can commit yourself to looking after your kitten for its entire life. For some people, once a kitten grows into an adult, it loses its novelty value. Every year the RSPCA rehomes over 35,000 cats who have been abadoned or badly treated by owners who didn't think carefully before taking their pet on. Kittens look cute and cuddly, but they may not be the best choice for all cat owners-to-be. Before taking on a kitten, consider the following points.

Some people say that anyone can own a cat. This is just not true. Certain individuals just aren't suited to living with a cat of any sort. Are you one of them? No matter how much you may love cats, affection alone will not keep a cat fit and healthy. Equally, it's not essential to have a big bank balance, a large house and a huge garden in order to be a cat's best friend. What you do need, however, is commitment – and plenty of it. You must be prepared to put your cat first and to make personal sacrifices for him. The following points and questions will help you decide whether you have got what it takes.

Cats who have free and unlimited access to the outdoors are, to a large extent, able to choose for themselves the kind of lifestyle they would like to lead. For me, that is what makes cats such brilliant pets. Most of the pet animals that people keep have little or no choice about what they do, when they do it or where they go to do it. But not all cats get such freedom of choice. Many longer-haired cats have coats that are not well-suited to the great outdoors. Some owners live in high-rise apartments. No matter what kind of cat you choose and no matter how independent a lifestyle he ends up leading, he will still be dependent on you and any other humans he lives with for nourishment, protection, shelter, education and healthcare. And when he is ill or injured, he will rely on you to save his life.

Below are just some of the things you need to think about before you become a cat owner:
• **Food** – Far from being just another mouth to feed, a kitten will have special nutritional needs. Despite the wide availability on supermarket shelves of pre-prepared cat foods, you will need to think very carefully about how to satisfy his dietary requirements. It takes more than the ability to open a tin to feed a cat properly.
• **Education** – Cats are born with the instincts of a free-living wild animal. Your kitten will need your help to adjust to a normal lifestyle. When you collect him at around eight weeks old he should have learnt a lot about being

a cat, about the houses we live in and the sometimes strange things people do. Although you will not need to train him to sit, come and stay in the same way you would a dog, he must learn from you what is acceptable behaviour and what is not.

• **Exercise** – Although cats spend more time sleeping each day than many other animals, all cats need physical and mental exercise to stay fit and healthy. If you decide to keep your cat restricted indoors or only give him limited access outside in a proper outdoor cage, you will need to provide him with games and furnishings that stimulate both his body and brain.

• **Healthcare** – Cats don't just stay healthy, you have to keep them that way. They need regular vaccinations, parasite control, dental care and grooming. Some of it you can do at home yourself. Other treatments will need to be done at a vet centre. Medical care for cats is now almost as sophisticated as it is for people. Not surprisingly, it can be expensive. Accidents and illness can happen at any time and some cats develop long-term problems that need years of treatment. Can you cope with the emotional and financial strain of unexpected major medical care? Are you prepared to nurse your cat when he is sick?

• **Holidays** – Who will look after your kitten when you are away on business or for pleasure?

• **Finances** – You may be able to afford to keep a cat now, but what will happen if your circumstances suddenly change? No one can see into the future, but you should think about what will happen to your cat if, for example, you are made redundant.

• **Other members of your family** – Even if you plan to be entirely responsible for caring for your new kitten, he will still interact with all the other members of your family. Do they like cats as much as you do? Although you may be desperate to own a kitten, are you in the minority? Inevitably, while he's learning the rules, your kitten will damage your property. How will you and your family react if he decides to scratch your new sofa with his claws? Will you all accept with good humour the odd hairs in your food when he is moulting? What about muddy paw-prints on your clothes, the carpet and the furniture when he dashes in through the cat flap on a wet day? There are some people who just cannot cope with crises like these. Will your kitten have to live with someone who will consider these predictable events major disasters? If so, the cat's life could be made a misery. If you invite a cat to live with you, you must welcome him wholeheartedly, muddy paws and all!

• **Legal responsibilities** – As a cat-owner you will be legally responsible for your cat's health and welfare.

Important health note: Some individuals are seriously allergic to cats. If you think that you or a member of your family may react badly to the presence of a cat in the house, talk to your doctor.

Other useful things to do:
• **Look back through your diary** – How would owning a cat have affected the entries in it?
• **Talk to cat-owning friends** – They will give you an honest opinion about both the down- and the up-sides of cat ownership.
• **Prepare a mock budget** – Create a list of all the bits and pieces you will need to set yourself up as a cat-owner. Then work out the 'running costs' of a typical cat. Remember to include food, vaccinations, parasite control products, healthcare/ insurance, cattery fees, grooming fees, replacement costs for worn-out toys, equipment and, of course, gifts and presents! Pick the brains of the staff at a local vet centre and pet accessory store.
• **Think ahead** – Your kitten will probably live longer than ten years. Try to think now of how your life may change in that time. If your circumstances alter you should be prepared to make provision for the cat in the same way you would for any other members of your family.

Choosing a cat

Your next task is to decide what sort of cat would suit you best. There are many different types of cats to choose from that vary in their appearance and temperament. Even though you may already be attracted to a certain breed or type of cat because of its looks, don't forget to consider its behavioural quirks and any special care needs it may have. For instance, Siamese cats are beautiful animals, but they are generally noisy, being fond of the sound of their own voices. Long-haired cats require much more intensive hair-care than their shorter-coated cousins. Your aim now should be to do some investigative research to find out more about the different types of cat that are available. Now is also the time to decide whether you want a kitten or an older cat and whether a male or female.

There are so many different types of cat to choose from that it is a good idea to try and classify them in some way.

Pure-bred and cross-bred cats

The advantage of choosing a pure-bred kitten is that you will have a good idea what your cat will look like and perhaps what his temperament will be when he is an adult. He should turn out to be similar in looks to his parents, his grandparents and even his great grandparents. But many people, including me, prefer cats of mixed breeds. A cat is referred to as a cross-breed if both his parents were pure breeds but of different types. New breeds of cat are usually made by breeding similar-looking cross-bred cats together for many generations until the kittens in a litter and their parents all resemble each other. The mysteries of genetics are such that there are no guarantees that a cross-bred kitten will resemble one parent more than the other.

Moggies

A cat may be called a moggie if one or both of his parents are cross-breeds (or moggies) themselves. With a moggie kitten, it can be difficult to predict exactly how big he will be, what he will look like or what kind of character he will have when he is fully grown – his parentage may have been mixed over several generations. The majority of pet cats in the UK are thought to be cross-breeds or moggies. They may not have 'blue' blood but they are no less special for that. Cross-bred cats and moggies are not second-class citizens in the feline world. In fact, when it comes to health matters, cross-bred cats may be fitter and hardier than their pure-bred parents.

A comprehensive study of the different cat breeds and types is essential if you are to identify the right kind of cat for you and your family. Remember, looks are not everything. Books on cat breeds will give you some idea of typical characteristics, but individual entries are often written by people with a vested interest in a particular breed and the information contained within them is often rather biased, I think.

In addition to reading books on cats, go and talk to the people who live and work with cats of all different kinds. Ask the opinions of your vet and the nurses at your vet centre and don't forget to speak to other owners, animal behaviour experts, trainers and even professional groomers. They will all have some interesting and very valid views on this important subject.

The following are other important things that you should consider carefully before setting about finding your new pet:

• **One cat or two ?** – If you are a busy person or family and you are concerned about the amount of time your cat may end up spending alone, you may think that getting two kittens is a good idea, as they will then have each other for company. In many cases that is true, but you must accept the possibility that the two kittens you take on may end up only tolerating each other, rather than actively enjoying each other's company. It may be best to choose two kittens from the same litter that seem to get on well. Some pet cats definitely prefer their own company, while others actively seek out friends. Even two loners will normally get along fine, as long as there is enough food and space for them to get away from each other when they want to. At first, as they are both the same kind of animal and speak the same language, the two kittens may bond with each other more strongly than they will with you. But as they get older, they may begin to challenge each other over resources such as food and sleeping areas in your house. If they are different genders, they will also try to mate if you do not get them neutered early enough! If you decide to take on two kittens remember that you are taking on double the responsibility and double the cost.

• **Male or female?** – Adult male un-neutered cats are stocky, thick-set individuals that are usually more active and destructive than females. They tend to roam, urine-mark and defend large territories. As a result, they are often involved in fights with other cats. Neutering males is the best way to help control such macho behaviour. On first meeting a cat that has been neutered before puberty, it can be difficult to tell from its outward appearance (without looking under its tail!) or behaviour whether it is male or female. Neutered males tend to behave more like females.

• **Young or old?** – The best age to bring a young kitten home is when he is eight weeks old. But you may want to consider taking on a well-socialised older kitten or adult cat. Taking on a young kitten may well be the best option for most families that have not had a cat before, as it is both fun and very educational to witness the development of a kitten into a fully grown cat.

Where to find a cat

Once you have decided what type of cat you want, you can start looking for possible places you might be able to obtain a suitable one. If you have decided that you would like a pure-bred cat or kitten, you should contact the secretary of the relevant breed club, or ask at your local rescue centre or vet surgery. Pure-bred adult cats are much less common residents at rescue centres than their cross-bred and moggie cousins, but it might be worth letting your local rescue centre know what you are after so that they can keep your name on file and let you know when a cat of the breed you are interested in becomes available for adoption.

If you want a cross-bred or moggie kitten then look in the classified sections of your local papers for advertisements, either for litters that are due or for newly born kittens. Contact the vet centres and animal rescue organisations in your area. They may be looking after, or may know of, a pregnant queen or one that has had kittens recently. If not, they should put you on a waiting list. If possible, visit several pregnant queens to meet them and their owners. Your choice may be limited in your area. If none of the queens on your initial shortlist meet your expectations, don't take the best of a bad bunch. Be patient and keep looking or begin to search further afield. Rescue centres may also have orphaned kittens, like Chocolate Chip, that need homes.

If you decide that you would like to take on an adult cross-bred or moggie cat I would urge you to visit your local rescue centre. There are so many adult cats needing good new homes. You will have met some of them on *Pet Rescue* if you are a regular viewer. But don't dive in and adopt any old cat or kitten just because you feel sorry for him or her. You, your home and your lifestyle may be totally unsuited to his or her needs. Always ask for expert guidance from the staff at the centre and spend as much time as you can with the cat you like before making any final decision.

WARNING

Never even think about obtaining a kitten from a pet shop, market or anywhere else that claims to sell a wide range of different breeds. Such places are usually unsuitable environments for kittens to live in, even for a short period. What's more, kittens sold from such places are likely to have had an appalling start in life.

Before collecting your new kitten or adult cat, make sure that you are fully prepared for his arrival home. That includes having made your house and garden safe for him, having bought all the necessary care equipment that you will need and having planned his diet and bought in supplies. Do not under any circumstances think about obtaining your cat and all his paraphernalia at the same time. If you plan your new pet's homecoming well in advance you will make this big event in his life as stress-free as possible and that will help him to settle in quickly.

Make an appointment for your new cat or kitten to be examined at your vet centre on the way home from collecting him. Your vet will make sure that he is fit and healthy and if there is something wrong you will benefit from expert advice immediately.

If you are not already registered with a vet centre you should carefully choose the one that you would like to attend well in advance. Every vet centre is different. Avoid choosing the one that is closest to you just because it is handy. Another local centre may be better suited to you and your new pet. Visit all the centres convenient to you. Chat to the staff and ask if you can have a guided tour of each centre. Take heed of your gut instincts, but also listen to the experiences and opinions of other pet owners.

Chocolate Chip makes mischief – as usual. His owner, Mandy, who works in the cattery at RSPCA Millbrook, says, 'He's got a brilliant character and is absolutely wonderful.'

'Cat flu' – what is it and what can you do to protect your cat?

More accurately, cat flu is called feline upper respiratory tract disease and is a common infectious condition suffered by cats, particularly in situations where lots of cats are kept together or brought together – for instance, boarding catteries, breeding colonies and cat rescue centres.

Although there may be a number of different infectious microscopic organisms involved in causing cat flu, by far the most important are two viruses called feline herpesvirus (FHV), also known as felinerhinotracheitis virus (FRV), and feline calicivirus (FCV). A cat will usually become infected by coming into direct contact with another cat suffering from cat flu. But as many cats continue to carry these viruses after they have recovered from infection, a cat may also become infected by direct contact with a cat that is apparently healthy at the time but has suffered from cat flu in the past. Both viruses will survive for a short time in the environment, and objects such as feeding bowls may also become sources of infection.

Symptoms

The precise symptoms shown by a cat with flu will vary depending on the specific cause and his immune system's ability to cope with the infection. FHV often causes severe symptoms. FCV may not result in any symptoms or may produce symptoms similar to FHV infection, depending on the strain of the virus involved. The following are all typical symptoms of cat flu:

- **Lack of appetite**
- **Fever**
- **Dullness and depression**
- **Sneezing**
- **Reddened, inflamed eyes** – They may become cloudy.
- **Nasal discharge (runny nose)** – Watery at first, then becoming thick and gungy.
- **Coughing** – Occasionally.
- **Tongue ulcers** – Especially with FCV infection.

All cats are at risk from cat flu. Although affected cats can be seriously ill, most recover. Severely affected very young or old individuals may die as a result of cat flu. Cats that do recover may go on to suffer from long-term problems such as rhinitis (inflammation of the nasal passages).

If your cat starts sneezing or shows any of the other symptoms listed above, keep him indoors and arrange for him to be examined at your vet centre. Prompt and appropriate treatment is essential to help prevent the short- and long-term complications of cat flu.

Your vet may be able to confirm that your cat is suffering from cat flu just by examining him, but he may not be able to tell which of the two main viruses are involved. If it is necessary to find out, he will take a swab from the back of your cat's throat and send it to a laboratory for analysis.

Treatment of cat flu

As there are no anti-viral medicines in common use, treatment of cat flu is based on a regime of good nursing, to encourage affected cats to continue eating and drinking, and the use of medicines to help alleviate symptoms. Your cat may require any or all of the following if he suffers from cat flu:

- **Medicines called mucolytics** to help break down and clear the build-up of mucus in your cat's respiratory system.
- **The administration of multi-vitamin preparations** to help stimulate appetite.
- **The administration of fluids** by intravenous drip to dehydrated cats.
- **The administration of liquid food** through tubes to cats that will not eat.

If your cat is seriously ill, he may need to be admitted as an in-patient for intensive care. If you are happy, willing and able to nurse your cat at home, your vet may prefer that you do so as your cat will probably be happier at home and he will be more likely to eat in a familiar environment. The nurse in charge of your cat's out-patient care will advise you of everything you will need to do for him. Your duties may include:

- **Cleaning away any discharges** from your cat's eyes and nose.
- **Keeping him warm and rested** – He must stay indoors.
- **Encouraging your cat to eat and drink**

Once your cat has suffered from cat flu, you must assume that he may be a carrier of the virus that infected him. Eight out of ten cats infected with FHV become lifelong virus carriers. But if your cat was infected by FHV he is only likely to be infectious to other cats intermittently, particularly if he is stressed either mentally or physically – such as by another disease, or through the mental anxiety associated with going into a cattery or moving house. At these times he will shed the virus into the environment, but may or may not suffer symptoms of cat flu. If he has been infected by FCV he is very likely to permanently shed the virus into the environment for a short time, although he may continue to do so for up to two years. If you do not know which virus your cat was infected with, you must assume either virus may have been involved.

Try to ensure that after recovering from cat flu, your cat leads as stress-free a life as possible. Show cats that have suffered from cat flu should be retired from the catwalk. If your cat has had cat flu in the past and she is now pregnant, you should ask your vet for specific advice on how to cope.

Protecting your cat

You should make sure that your cat is regularly and routinely vaccinated against both FHV and FCV. Most vaccines against these two viruses will not actually prevent your cat from becoming infected, or reduce the chance of him becoming a virus-carrier after recovery from infection, but they will significantly reduce the severity of the disease that your cat will suffer should he become infected.

Normally, vaccinations against FHV and FCV are combined with other vaccinations as part of a vaccination regime that involves two doses three to four weeks apart to start with and then a booster dose at twelve-month intervals from then on. The precise regime recommended by your vet will depend on the products that he uses. New-born kittens receive some protection against these viruses naturally from their mother, but the protection is only short-lived, so vaccination is important. In most cases, they are ready to receive the first dose of their primary vaccination course when they are between six and twelve weeks old.

Cats that have suffered from cat flu should still be vaccinated regularly, as natural immunity as a result of real infection does not last long. What's more, there are many strains of FCV.

The greyhound: a gentle but much-maligned animal

THE FIRST TIME I MET DUCHESS, SHE CAME UP TO ME AND STUCK HER BIG, POINTY WET NOSE RIGHT DOWN MY EAR HOLE. SHE IS A WONDERFUL DOG. LIKE ALMOST EVERY GREYHOUND I HAVE EVER HAD THE PLEASURE TO KNOW, SHE LOVES PEOPLE AND IS GENTLE, SWEET-NATURED AND INCREDIBLY LAID BACK WITH ME AND EVERY ONE ELSE WHO BOTHERS TO SAY HELLO TO HER. SHE HAS THE MOST ENDEARING EXPRESSION, AND AS I WRITE THESE WORDS I CAN PICTURE HER BIG, ROUND EYES STARING AT ME THROUGH HER KENNEL DOOR. THE STORIES IN THIS CHAPTER ARE FOR THE MANY PEOPLE WHO HAVE SEEN GREYHOUND RACING AND HAVE MISCONCEPTIONS ABOUT GREYHOUNDS.

The greyhound is one of the oldest breeds of dog, thought to date back over 8,000 years. Amazingly, despite the fact that people have lived with greyhounds for thousands of years, these wonderful dogs still suffer from being misunderstood. Some people think of greyhounds as fast, aggressive animals with bared teeth showing through their muzzles as they chase an electronic hare around a racetrack. This image is a far cry from the placid, gentle, loving and often lazy dogs which typify the breed. They can make wonderful pets for the right kind of owner.

Duchess and Earl

The RSPCA centre at Great Ayton near Middlesbrough is close to a number of greyhound racing tracks in north-east England, and is consequently offered an endless stream of unwanted dogs whose racing careers are over. Because greyhounds are notoriously difficult to rehome, Maggie Eden, Great Ayton's manager, admits to keeping the number she is prepared to take in down to a minimum. She says: 'People want cute, fluffy dogs and greyhounds are big, leggy and skinny. People think of

greyhounds as racing dogs and not as pets to curl up with at home.' However, greyhounds Duchess and Earl came to Great Ayton not because their racing careers were over, but because they had been all but abandoned. They were being kept on an allotment and had attracted the attention of concerned neighbours who could see that they were living in filthy conditions.

The RSPCA received two separate reports that the dogs were in a terrible state and needed rescuing. They were kept in a muddy-floored shed where the north wind blew in through an open doorway. RSPCA Inspector Ian Jackson described the state of the dogs: 'They were very thin and very weak. It was extremely cold and they were shivering and miserable with only a wet cushion to sleep on. Earl had two painful sores on his back and sores on his legs. Some of their skin had worn away from lying on a hard surface. They were horrifyingly underweight, probably close to starvation.'

Duchess and Earl were owned by the same man, or at least had been until he grew bored and left them in the care of a girlfriend. She claimed to be looking after the dogs, but according to Ian Jackson, 'It was clear

Duchess at home with Jill Dean, Mop and one of Jill's pointers. The right diet has transformed Duchess from the thin, unhappy dog on the opposite page

from their condition that she didn't have a clue. She wasn't a bad kid, just young and had absolutely no idea of how to care for the dogs.' The woman has since been successfully prosecuted – fined £200, ordered to pay £100 costs and banned from custody of animals for three years. It was suspected that in this case, as in many others, the greyhounds had been bought with the intention of racing them without any thought for the time and commitment that this entails. Although Earl bore an identification tattoo common to racing dogs, it had obviously been some time since he had been with a proper trainer or had any expert care.

Earl and Duchess were taken to the RSPCA centre at Great Ayton. Thanks to the loving attention of the staff and proper veterinary care, the dogs recovered well. With correct feeding Earl, white with grey markings, went from a pitiful 18kg (2 stone 11 lbs) to 27kg (4 stone 3 lbs), and Duchess, a lovely blue-grey, managed to reach 23kg (3 stone 8 lbs), an increase of 7kg (just over a stone) on her arrival weight. Maggie Eden believes that: 'Often, out of ignorance, people keep greyhounds underweight in the belief that they will run faster if they are hungry. This is not true. Hungry greyhounds are debilitated and weak.'

Until the RSPCA prosecution was completed, the dogs could not be rehomed. The situation was unavoidable, but of course the dogs did not understand this. Duchess and Earl were becoming dejected. Earl's more outgoing, lively temperament was helping him to cope, but Duchess, more sedate in character, was beginning to display symptoms of kennel stress (see page 62). She was jumping up and down repeatedly and turning round and round in her kennel, and she split her tail from continually lashing it against the walls. Despite all the efforts of the RSPCA vet, the tail would not heal and eventually it had to be amputated.

In a final bid to find homes for Duchess and Earl, Maggie enlisted the help of the local press. A short piece with accompanying photographs duly appeared in the *Middlesbrough Gazette*, and after a few days a man came forward showing an interest in Earl. The staff were encouraged that finally the dogs' fortunes were turning. Unfortunately, after several days, the man came back with the sad news that his landlord had refused to grant permission for him to keep a dog. Duchess and Earl were back to square one.

Because of the many misconceptions about the breed, people are afraid to offer homes to greyhounds. It is important to remember that not all greyhounds have been trained for the track. In general they make great pets

— for the right people. Ex-racers need very special care and retraining to help them adjust to life off the track, where small furry creatures are more often cherished than chased. Although the RSPCA finds that the greyhound is the hardest breed to rehome, they are not generally returned to RSPCA centres once they have found a loving family as the gentleness and loyalty of the breed mean the affection of new owners is assured. Contrary to popular belief, greyhounds do not need a lot of exercise and can in fact be lazier than many other dogs. Even though they are big, they are lightweight, they don't have huge appetites and their short coats do not need much grooming. Most are tolerant of children and other dogs, though ex-racers can be lively and a bit of a handful and need committed owners.

Animal behavioural counsellor Sarah Whitehead says of the greyhound: 'The nature/nurture debate with greyhounds is a very difficult one, and it is almost impossible to say how much of their chasing behaviour is pre-wired genetically in the brain of the animal and how much is the responsibility of its training once it begins a racing career. It all comes down to the specific animal, but we can probably safely say that with training they become better practised at chasing. Some greyhounds will never want to chase another animal once they are rehomed, but also it would be true to say that there are dogs who will never not want to chase them in the first place. You have to use common sense and match the individual dog to the

Duchess runs over the moors in Yorkshire. Her similarity to the dogs seen in engravings at ancient Egyptian sites is striking

Bambi is another happily rehomed greyhound. This characteristic pose shows her gentle temperament

right household. It is probably better not to house greyhounds in homes with rabbits, guinea pigs or hamsters – anything small and fast-moving could trigger their chase response. The most important factor is to make sure that the greyhound is socialised with other dogs, as this will go a long way to preventing him from chasing other animals.'

Because the RSPCA likes to make every possible effort to rehome 'difficult' animals, Earl was transferred in the animal ambulance to the RSPCA centre at Millbrook in Chobham, Surrey. RSPCA centres in the south of England have significantly higher rehoming rates than those in the north but even so, Millbrook was unwilling to take Duchess as well because staff were less optimistic about the likelihood of rehoming two greyhounds. The staff at Great Ayton hoped that Duchess and Earl would not miss each other because they had always been kennelled separately.

Maggie Eden was optimistic about Earl's chances at Millbrook, but unfortunately, his chasing tendencies were proving to be a problem. Sue Walters, Millbrook's deputy manager says, 'Earl had a very strong urge to chase other animals, especially cats. He lunged at our resident cat,

George, when George was sitting completely still on a chair, and was also aggressive towards other dogs. Once he'd fixed his attention on something, there was nothing we could do to distract him.' Millbrook staff worked with Earl to try to train him out of his bad habits by trying to find something that would interest him more than cats, but couldn't help him. Says Sue, 'Nothing would break his very intense concentration – we tried treats, toys and everything we could think of.' In the end, manager Tony Glue took the view that Earl was not suitable for rehoming, and made the very difficult decision to put him to sleep. Sue comments that Earl's case is unusual: 'Earl was one of only two greyhounds that we've had to put down over a period of several years, and we rehome most greyhounds very successfully, but he really did have a serious problem.'

Meanwhile, Duchess's photograph had been spotted in the *Middlesbrough Gazette* by a woman whose twelve-year-old greyhound, Ziggy, had recently died. Jill Dean lives on the Yorkshire Moors where she looks after five dogs – three red setters and two pointers – for the owner of the racehorse Desert Orchid. Jill and her son, both dog lovers, have a seven-year-old long-haired Jack Russell called Mop. Ziggy had been rescued from racing kennels and had become a much loved member of the family. Jill is enthusiastic about the breed: 'People just don't understand how wonderful and gentle greyhounds are. I must admit, I didn't either until I got Ziggy, but I never want to be without one now.'

Jill's initial visit to Great Ayton to meet Duchess went well, but when she returned with Mop, Duchess snapped. Says Maggie Eden, 'It was very unlike Duchess to snap, but I think it was simply a result of being locked in kennels for a year without contact with other dogs. So when Mop turned up and started sniffing her bottom, of course she snapped.' Maggie and the staff at Great Ayton subsequently carried out some tests on Duchess to gauge her reaction to other dogs. They let her run around the compound muzzled and then after a little while, removed the muzzle and were delighted to find that Duchess played well with the other dogs. 'It was a one-off incident with Mop, so we rang Jill Dean and told her the good news,' says Maggie. Indeed, when Jill returned with Mop and Duchess was taken off the leash, the two dogs were quite friendly towards one another. At last, Duchess had found a new owner.

Duchess has adjusted very well to her new home and her new canine companions. All seven dogs go for long walks across the moors every day – the kind of lifestyle Duchess could only have dreamed of. Though Duchess enjoys these long walks, Jill is quick to point out that they are not strictly necessary for her continued health. 'In general, greyhounds are very placid, lazy dogs who like a quick burst of activity, but don't have a lot of stamina.'

Jill adopted Duchess in late 1996. She says that, 'Within a very short time, she began to relax and enjoy the affection we gave her. She wouldn't say boo to a goose now. Initially she was just a little bit nervous of being in a new home, but I knew she would come round as soon as she realised we loved her and weren't going to hurt her.' Thanks to Jill's experience with dogs, she was not unduly worried by Duchess's slightly timid temperament. After several weeks adjusting to her new home, Duchess abandoned all her defences and is now a beautiful blue-grey 'couch-potato' who loves a cuddle.

When I visited their home, Duchess was asleep on the sofa with Mop. Amazingly, Jill was sitting on the floor to give the dogs more room! She explained that although Mop is definitely the boss, the dogs are not competitive and often curl up together. Duchess's relationship with Mop is living proof that not all greyhounds chase anything smaller than them – in fact, many are capable of forming close friendships with other animals.

According to Jill, 'Duchess might have her interest aroused when she sees a cat, but she can always be called back. I believe that dogs are more likely to attack when they are on the lead than off, because they feel they cannot defend themselves if they are tethered and don't like to feel restricted.'

The history of the racing greyhound

Archaeological remains show that the greyhound existed in the Middle East several thousand years ago, where it was a highly favoured animal. These ancient dogs were the companions of princes and in Egypt their images are engraved on the tombs of the pharaohs. They have been used as sporting dogs for at least 2,000 years, and the first apologist for hare-coursing, Flavius Arrianus, a Roman citizen, described the aim of the sport: 'The true sportsman does not take out his dogs to destroy the hares but for the sake of the course and the contest between the dogs and hares, and is glad if the hare escapes.'

In Britain from the eleventh to eighteenth centuries the sport was the province of royalty and the nobility. King Canute, whose laws in 1014 set aside vast tracts of land for the hunting pleasure of the wealthier classes, decided that: 'No meane person may keep any greyhound.' Dogs found in the ownership of the lower orders had their feet mutilated to prevent them from hunting. Such harsh measures at least ensured that the breed survived. Coursing flourished throughout the Middle Ages, and the late Tudors turned it into a competitive sport from which the greyhound racing we know today descended.

The Victorian era saw a great boom in coursing, as it became more accessible to the manufacturing classes, who had leisure time, money, and the means of travelling to meetings – the steam train. The hares would be driven out of scrubland, where the dogs would chase them for as far as three miles before becoming exhausted. Crowds and numbers of owners grew, and vast sums were spent on breeding, rearing and training greyhounds. Most puppies were reared on remote hills with complete freedom to roam. Extensive exercise, a good diet, and nights spent sheltering in barns made fit, very tough dogs. Rearing continued in this fashion until the 1950s when the increase in road traffic made it impossible, even in the remotest areas.

Track racing, which began in 1876, began to take over from open coursing, and hit a peak in Britain in the 1930s. It is still a very popular sport, and today there are thirty-five National Greyhound Racing Club registered dog tracks in England and Scotland with over 10,000 dogs registered to race every year. There are also fifty independent tracks.

Training a champion usually begins when the dog is six months old. The pups are housed at the training grounds and are walked daily on hard surfaces. Trainers believe that exercising puppies like this strengthens their feet and that this is important because greyhounds with weak feet can never become racers – they lose precious distance at the start of any race. I don't suppose that's ever been proven! At fifteen months greyhounds begin short racing trials at the tracks. Bred for speed and not stamina, the greyhound is encouraged to run as quickly as possible for a very short distance; a far cry from the days when it would chase across downland for miles and miles.

Obviously, not all greyhounds bred for racing make it. And even for those that do, what happens when they stop winning? The average racing dog – and even a champion – is retired when he is three to five years old. Although still young, he is no longer of any use, and is without a home. Growing concern for the fate of the retired greyhound within the racing industry has led to the establishment of organisations that exist to find homes for dogs who have finished their racing careers, most notably the

Retired Greyhound Trust (RGT) in Worcester Park, Surrey, run by the National Greyhound Racing Committee (NGRC).

In addition, there are grave concerns for the fate of dogs that fail to reach champion status. Many are sold for £50 to £100, and go on to run at one of the fifty independent tracks in the UK. The racing is not conducted under the very stringent NGRC rules, and a vet is not always in attendance to help injured dogs.

Greyhounds as pets

Director of the RGT David Poole is adamant that all greyhounds, racing dogs or not, should be given a second chance. 'The nature of the breed is affectionate, docile and sensitive. These qualities combine with the firm discipline already instilled from their racing careers to help make the transition smooth. Many retired greyhounds are kept by owners and trainers into their old age, but those who are not can be helped by us.' The RGT runs over thirty schemes to rehome greyhounds at racetracks round the UK, and in 1996 the charity rehomed 1,262 dogs. David suggests that the greyhound is becoming a popular pet dog as the myths about the breed are slowly put to rest.

If you would like more information on adopting a greyhound you can visit your local animal rescue centre to see if they have any available for rehoming or contact the RGT (see page 127), who will put you in touch with your local scheme. It costs nothing to adopt a greyhound from the RGT, though sometimes new owners make a donation for the running costs. Prospective owners should expect a home visit before a dog can be adopted.

And finally...

Not all greyhounds looking for homes are ex-racing dogs. Some were always intended as family pets, like Bambi, a friendly, tan greyhound. She was brought into RSPCA Millbrook in October 1996 because her owners were moving to a smaller house and didn't think there would be enough room for a dog. Because she was not a racing dog, she was easier to rehome than most greyhounds, and was soon adopted by Lynn Stock and her daughter Anna in Esher, Surrey. Her new owners are delighted. Says Lynn: 'She's been brilliant, well-behaved, docile; she's very good. Just a couple of times she has run away, but at least she always runs home.'

Bambi, a placid, friendly dog, at home with owner Lynn Stock

A tale of two goats

AFTER MANY YEARS OF TREATING ONLY PETS, I'VE RECENTLY STARTED WORK IN A VETERINARY PRACTICE THAT CARES FOR ALL CREATURES GREAT AND SMALL. I FEEL LIKE JAMES HERRIOT! MY FIRST FARM-ANIMAL PATIENTS WERE QUINTUPLETS – FIVE ADORABLE GOAT KIDS PROUDLY OWNED BY A WOMAN WHO IS GOAT CRAZY. I ALWAYS ENJOY SEEING HER BECAUSE I LOVE GOATS AND EVERY TIME WE MEET WE JUST CHEW THE CUD AND CHAT GOAT, MUCH TO THE AMUSEMENT OF MY COLLEAGUES, ESPECIALLY THE VETERINARY NURSES. ASK ANYONE WHO SPENDS TIME WITH AND REALLY UNDERSTANDS GOATS AND THEY'LL TELL YOU THAT THEY ARE WONDERFUL CREATURES WITH VERY SPECIAL NEEDS.

Loxley and Rainbow: a love story

Loxley and Rainbow's unusual romance is one of the strangest the *Pet Rescue* team have come across. They were rescued, separately, by the RSPCA from very unhappy circumstances, but they became inseparable at Great Ayton in Yorkshire.

Rainbow, a billy goat, was spotted tethered to a hedgerow by a man walking along a bridlepath. The man thought that Rainbow looked distressed, and could see a deep wound in his neck caused by the rope and heavy chain that prevented him from moving far.

In response to the man's phone call, Inspector Ian Jackson rescued Rainbow and brought him to RSPCA Great Ayton. From looking at Rainbow's teeth – the standard way of trying to assess a goat's age – Ian judged him to be about ten years old. Around his neck was bailing twine attached to a chain weighing more than 2.5 kilos (5-6 lb). This chain was so heavy that the twine had cut an inch into poor Rainbow's neck. To compound matters, tar had been poured over the wound, presumably as a misguided attempt at first aid. Tethering a goat without access to shelter or the freedom to move around and browse for food is cruel in the extreme.

With loving care from the staff at Great Ayton, Rainbow soon began to recover. He was put on a special diet to help him regain weight, and the tar

was cut away from around the wound on his neck and treated with antiseptic solutions. This, combined with a nutritionally balanced diet, meant that his wound healed quickly. Rainbow also received treatment for lice, and his coat soon took on a healthy sheen. Within weeks he was in much better shape.

Billy goats can be more than a bit headstrong, but Rainbow's reluctance to be friendly to the staff at Great Ayton was no doubt worsened by his ill-treatment and the time he had spent alone. However, during his recovery process something unusual helped to soften the angry billy goat's heart. RSPCA staff noticed a strange romance blossoming in the paddock. Rainbow was spending all his time with a young bullock called Loxley.

Loxley had also suffered greatly before he arrived at Great Ayton, and his owner was successfully prosecuted. Loxley was found in a squalid farm building with a number of other calves, some of which were dead. Out of desperation, because they were starving to death, Loxley and the surviving calves – naturally all herbivores, who normally eat only plant matter – were trying to eat the dead animals. From the original group, Loxley is the only one to have survived the trauma.

Rainbow enjoys his new freedom in Yorkshire. His injury has completely healed and the days of being constantly tethered are firmly in the past

Sue Carr sometimes takes Rainbow for a walk on the Yorkshire Moors, and at home he is free to wander as he pleases

Loxley and Rainbow played together, walked together, ate together and lay down at night together. The pair became so attached that when the time came for adoption, Maggie Eden decided that they had to be rehomed together. After forming such a loving bond, it would have been heartless to split them up.

There are few people committed or capable enough to take on both a goat and a bullock and so Maggie appealed to Sue Carr, a stalwart member of the local community who had already adopted several animals (one lamb, three nanny goats, two billy goats and seven goat kids) from RSPCA Great Ayton. Sue, now a farmer, is a former sixth-form college teacher who moved from London in 1974 in search of a quieter life. She has lived on Danby Dale on the Yorkshire Moors for the last five years with her husband, also a teacher. Since moving to Eastfield Farm Sue has gradually increased her livestock, having started off with just a few ducks, one goose and two goats.

She now has three sheep, seven geese, twenty-five goats… and a twelve-year-old son! They all live in the paddock together. (Except the son of course!) 'I particularly love goats because they have such individual characters,' says Sue. 'It's impossible to say that you know goats, because the minute you do, they'll turn round and do something completely unpredictable. Some of my herd are totally certifiable, but I love them all.'

There is no commercial purpose in the Carrs' farm: they simply love animals, and, through the milk they get from their goats, have introduced an element of self-sufficiency into their lives. Sue began milking the goats when she discovered she had an allergy to cows' milk. The goats are milked by hand once a day – which takes about ten minutes for each goat – and fed in the morning and evening. She lets the kids take what they want from their mothers and then she has what's left.

Sue cannot sell the milk as, in her words, 'goats-milk products are becoming as regulated as dairy products'. To milk goats commercially, Sue says you need a minimum of 100 goats, a very expensive stainless steel parlour, and the equipment to pasteurise the milk. Such large-scale production is not only financially impossible for Sue, but she also feels it would diminish the relationship she has with her goats. 'I like to talk to them while I'm milking, but if I had a commerical parlour, they would all be hooked up to machines and they would just be numbers. It would take all the fun out of it for me, and, besides, I'm not in it for the money.' Any left-over milk is frozen to use during the winter, when Sue likes to give the goats a rest from milking. What the family doesn't drink she turns into cheese: a soft camembert type, which takes four days to make, and a hard cheddar-like one, which is compressed for a week in a cheese press and then left to stand for three months.

Loxley and Rainbow settled in very well and spend most of their days wandering in the fields. 'They have a totally free rein,' says Sue, 'but can always get into the barn to shelter when the weather is bad and at night. There is hay in the hay rack and plenty of water for them. All in all, I'd say they have a pretty good life.'

About a month after he arrived, Sue had Loxley castrated on the advice of a neighbour who warned her that Friesian bulls could be very aggressive. 'I was told that he was likely to became very temperamental and so thought it prudent to get him done! I was worried that it might hurt him, but, frankly, he didn't bat an eyelid and gave no indication of any pain.'

Loxley is a bit of a Casanova! Not satisfied with one love, he soon struck up another romance with a goat called Holly, and at night he lies with Rainbow and Holly on either side. Loxley is a youngster and Sue looks forward to spending many happy years watching him romance her goats!

Gemini: it's worth waiting for the right home

Very few goats are as lucky as Rainbow. In fact, it is often difficult even to get them admitted to RSPCA centres because the time taken to rehome them means that all available space is already taken.

Chief Inspector Nicky Ramsey had been called out to Gemini's home because of a complaint that Gemini was suffering from neglect. He had lice, worms, almost no hair and was kept locked in a small garden shed all day, with dogs barking at him. When Nicky found him locked in his shed, the dogs were baying outside and Gemini was shaking with terror, almost frozen. Because Gemini was unused to being handled, Nicky had a job to coax Gemini out of the shed.

Gemini's owners were living in a small house with a frog, a snake, a rabbit, a chipmunk, nine cats, two dogs and a number of chickens. Because they liked animals, they had gradually accumulated this strange menagerie, but with little thought for the amount of time caring for the animals would take: the cats had been handled so little that they had become almost feral. To makes things worse, one of the owners was seriously ill, and they simply couldn't cope with their animals.

'They loved their animals,' says Nicky. 'But they just couldn't cope.' But even if the RSPCA wasn't about to mount a prosecution, Nicky certainly felt that they were guilty of foolhardiness. Their animals had suffered because the owners had not thought hard enough about how well they could care for such a large and diverse group. These animals have since been rehomed to responsible owners, but Nicky feels that the situation shouldn't have arisen in the first place. 'I see it every day and it makes me so angry,' she says. 'People just don't think.'

When Gemini first arrived at Millbrook he was in a sorry state, but he started to recover well. With companionship from the workers at Millbrook he calmed down and even became friendly. A correct diet enabled him to gain the weight he needed and his coat became long and lustrous. Gemini developed a special attachment to Andrew, one of the staff members at Millbrook. Sue Walters, the centre's deputy manager, says: 'Andrew formed a strong relationship with Gemini. Every day he would spend time just chatting with him and taking him for walks on a lead. It was really

touching and extremely beneficial for Gemini, who lost a lot of his aggression and actually became quite affectionate. When he first came in you couldn't go near him, but now he loves to have his head scratched and spend time with people.'

Gemini is an old man in goat terms, but he is still fit and strong. Obviously, no one can say how much longer he will live, but there's no doubt that he deserved to spend what time he had left in a loving home where he would certainly bring a great deal of pleasure to new owners. But, after he had been at Millbrook for ten months, the staff had almost given up hope. Then, in March 1997 they had a call from Barbara Harlow of Banstead, Surrey, who was desperately searching for a companion for her ten-month-old angora billy goat, Twiggs.

Barbara had begun keeping angora goats partly for their wool and partly as pets. She had also begun rescuing Shetland ponies about ten years previously and for the last five years has been breeding British spotted ponies. But slowly, more and more goats were added to her herd as she

Gemini before he was rehomed. His beautiful thick coat and healthy appearance are thanks to the hard work of the staff at RSPCA Millbrook

answered calls from people wanting to rehome them. 'The minute I started calling round looking for a friend for Twiggs, all these goats started coming out of the woodwork. I've gone from having three angora goats and one angora cross to thirteen goats in total – most of them rescue cases with behavioural problems through either neglect or ill-treatment. It's complete madness, but I've got the space and I'm happy to care for them all.'

Things didn't work out quite as planned for Gemini. When he was put in with Twiggs, Barbara realised that perhaps it wasn't wise to have two uncastrated males together. Gemini was quite aggressive towards Twiggs and has since been put with two females. 'He's as happy as a sandboy now,' says Barbara. 'Occasionally he gets a bit bolshie and hisses at us, but we just hiss right back and he's beginning to understand that we're not afraid of him, but also that he has nothing to fear from us. He's settled in very well.'

The RSPCA and the British Goat Society both recommend that uncastrated male goats should not be kept as pets, so Gemini's story is the exception rather than the rule. Barbara Harlow, who doesn't intend to breed from Gemini, is lucky enough to have the space to keep him, and doesn't mind his natural male characteristics, which potential goat-owners can find off-putting.

Susan Knowles of the British Goat Society says: 'Male goats do not make good pets: they smell, can be very aggressive if they're not handled correctly, and usually end up unwanted. I deal with unwanted male goats every day and it makes me angry as well as sad. It's a situation that can and should be avoided. All male goat kids that are destined to be kept as pets should be castrated and disbudded by a vet when they are very young – and then they do make good pets.' Disbudding means removing their horn buds so that they never grow – this avoids any accidents.

Goats as pets

As Gemini and Rainbow's stories prove, goats suffer both physically and emotionally if they are not loved and cared for properly. They are suitable pets only for people who have the space, time, money and commitment to ensure that they get the very best of care. If you would like to become a goat keeper then you should do your homework first and find out as much about goats as you possibly can. Don't just rely on books, get out and about and meet up with people who live with goats. A good place to find keen goat owners is at a county show. They love people who love goats, so if your affection for goats is genuine you will get on really well. Make sure that you join the British Goat Society (contact address on page 126).

The following will give you just a taste of the kinds of things you will need to consider in detail before taking on goats:

• **Types of goat** – The British Goat Society recommends that would-be pet goat owners consider only the following kinds of goat. (Whatever the type of goat, wethers – castrated males – are generally easier for pet owners to care for.)

Pygmies – small goats, originally from Africa. Probably the best kind of goat for keeping as a pet. But they are small enough to be good escape artists!

Dairy goats – Saanens, Toggenburgs, British Alpines, Anglo Nubians and Golden Guernseys … great names! Females from low-yielding breed lines can make good pets, but some goats are so-called maiden milkers – they will produce milk without being mated.

Fibre goats – Need a lot of hair care! Angoras are sheared twice a year.

Meat goats – The only one in this country is the Boer. Not many available.

Rare breeds – Bagots were around in the fourteenth century. Today their breeding is supervised by the Rare Breeds Survival Trust (see address on page 127).

• **Company** – Naturally, goats are very sociable creatures that prefer to live with others of their own kind, but they will make the most of any company they can get. In my opinion, they should never be kept alone.

• **Accommodation** – The more space they have the better. Assume that to keep even a small number of goats, you will need at least one acre divided up into a few smaller paddocks so that your goats can be moved between paddocks to prevent over-grazing and the build-up of harmful parasites. As goats are browsers as well as grazers, their paddocks should allow them plenty of opportunity to pick and choose how they spend their time. Grass paddocks can quickly become muddy in wet weather. Many breeds of goat are more sensitive to inclement weather than, for instance, cattle or sheep, and so must be given 24-hour access to a cosy and weatherproof shelter. However, the shelter should be as large as possible, the minimum floor space per goat should be around 2.5 square metres (3 square yards). They enjoy their creature comforts and must be given plenty of dry bedding. Goats jump and climb so all fencing needs to be very strong and at least 1.2 metres (4 feet) high. Goats should never be tethered.

• **Food and water** – Goats must have access to fresh, clean water at all times. They prefer it if it's not too cold! A female producing milk can easily drink around 20 litres (4.5 gallons) of water a day. Like all animals, goats need a good balanced diet that keeps them in tip-top condition. The precise diet for a goat will depend on its age and lifestyle. Growing kids and nannies in milk have special nutritional needs. Goats need a lot of bulky food to ensure that their digestive system works properly and even when they have access to grazing and browsing they should be offered as much good quality hay as they want. In addition, most need some so-called 'concentrates' to keep them fit and healthy. The widely held view is that goats can eat almost anything. They certainly have bizarre tastes – Gemini ate one of my scripts on one occasion! But seriously, they can be poisoned by some wild plants such as honeysuckle, yew or laburnum.

• **Healthcare** – Goats should be examined every day for signs of illness or injury. They need vaccinating every year and most need to have their hooves trimmed regularly.

Why not check out:

• 'Codes of recommendations for the welfare of livestock – Goats', a booklet available from the Ministry of Agriculture, Fisheries and Food (address on page 126).

• 'Goats', a booklet available from the RSPCA.

• A series of leaflets on goats and their care available from the British Goat Society.

Skippy and Miss Button: the perfect partnership

THIS MAY SOUND ODD, BUT I DON'T OFTEN GET TO SEE *PET RESCUE*. MOST DAYS I DON'T GET HOME UNTIL AT LEAST 7.30PM AND I'VE LONG SINCE GIVEN UP TRYING TO PROGRAMME THE VIDEO. I GET TO SEE MOST STORIES DURING THE PROCESS OF FILMING, BUT ONE I MISSED WAS THAT OF SKIPPY AND MISS BUTTON. THE FIRST I KNEW OF IT WAS AT CRUFTS WHEN I WAS ACCOSTED BY HORDES OF PEOPLE WANTING TO KNOW HOW THE TWO OF THEM WERE GETTING ON. UNUSUALLY FOR ME, I WAS COMPLETELY LOST FOR WORDS. SO I GOT HOLD OF A TAPE OF THE PROGRAMME TO SEE WHAT ALL THE FUSS WAS ABOUT. IT WAS IMMEDIATELY OBVIOUS. THERE IN FRONT OF ME WAS THE BEST ADVERTISEMENT FOR PET OWNERSHIP THAT ANYONE IS EVER LIKELY TO SEE.

Many *Pet Rescue* viewers will remember three-legged Skippy and her owner, retired schoolteacher Violet Button. Skippy's resolute character won Miss Button over the instant they met, and the dog's missing leg was no obstacle to a great friendship.

At the beginning of September 1996, the RSPCA centre at Great Ayton was contacted by a woman pleading with them to come and take her dog, a three-year-old terrier cross called Skippy, because she couldn't cope. A week previously, Skippy's leg had been amputated after an accident with a car. Great Ayton's manager, Maggie Eden, urged the woman to hold on to Skippy for a little while until she had completely recovered from surgery, but the owner was adamant that she could no longer care for her: 'I think that people are often frightened of disability,' says Maggie, 'in addition to which I'm not sure how committed she was to the dog. The fact that she let her stray in the first place – which led to the accident occurring – was very telling. I was concerned that Skippy might pick up an infection by being kennelled with other dogs so soon after major surgery, but in the end I had no option but to accept her.'

Skippy was extremely timid when she first arrived at the centre. Maggie says, 'She was so frightened that we used to have to put her food in her bed. Even though her leg had healed well and she could walk, she wouldn't leave her bed. She was such a sweet little dog, a lovely personality, incredibly trusting when you consider what she'd been through.' Poor Skippy, in the space of a week, had suffered the acute trauma of losing her leg, her owner and her home.

That Skippy survived these few weeks at all is testimony to her extraordinary physical strength and character. But as people are often very wary of disabled dogs, Maggie feared that rehoming her would be a problem. Skippy was in the kennels for several weeks and ready for a new home, but the arrival of a litter of pups next door was attracting a lot of attention, and finding someone willing to take her on wasn't going to be easy. Although people were arriving daily to look for dogs, Skippy was constantly passed over in favour of other dogs. Her future looked bleak.

Then Violet Button showed up. Miss Button was looking for another dog after her beloved Cairn terrier, Gemma, had died earlier in the year. Miss Button had always loved dogs, but her father was adamant that 'only blind men and shepherds should be allowed dogs' and so she waited until after her father's death before getting her first canine companion! Miss Button was extremely moved by Skippy's plight and they clicked instantly. Once the RSPCA's home-checking procedure had been completed, the decision to adopt Skippy was an easy one. 'I remember it clearly,' says Maggie, 'I kept saying to Miss Button, "Are you sure you don't want to take her for a walk to see how you get on?" but Miss Button kept replying, "No, I don't think I need to do that, thank you very much." It was really funny, she just wanted to get her in the car and take her home straight away. It was definitely love at first sight for those two.' They had a walk together and when Skippy was finally led out of her kennel into the car, Miss Button was heard to say, 'You're my little dog now, Skippy.'

'I knew immediately that she was the dog for me, a real companion; such a dear little thing and so trusting when you consider what she'd been through,' says Miss Button, who believes that a dog is a tremendous social boon in two ways. Not only do dogs provide wonderful companionship, but Miss Button finds people much more friendly towards her as a dog owner. 'If you're on your own, they can be suspicious, but the minute you have a dog with you, especially Skippy with only three legs, people just walk right up to you and start chatting. I find it especially gratifying that so many children take an interest in her. I think it's wonderful the way a dog can break down those barriers so quickly.'

Miss Button says that Skippy was quite insecure when she first brought her home and was constantly checking to see that her new owner hadn't disappeared. Given the traumatic nature of Skippy's recent experiences, this was perhaps not surprising. But she soon settled in happily and began showing typical terrier traits of inquisitiveness and alertness. Far from finding Skippy's disability a problem, Miss Button claims that on their walks across the Yorkshire Moors, 'She runs like a whippet – she's a real skippy!' Skippy behaves like any other playful, happy, healthy dog. The only difference is that occasionally Skippy will overbalance a little trying to correct for the lack of a back leg. Miss Button and Skippy are now devoted companions and she says, 'I hope we have many more years together.'

Skippy's missing leg is no obstacle to fun: she can run and play just like any four-legged dog, and enjoys long walks on the Yorkshire Moors

What's good for Miss Button may be good for you

The emotional and physical benefits of pet ownership, but particularly that of dogs, are legion. They are wonderful companions for anybody, especially the elderly and anyone living alone. They act as a social lubricant and ice-breaker as described by Miss Button. *The Waltham Book of Human–Animal Interaction* cites a number of studies conducted in the USA which show that walking a pet or sitting in a public place with a pet elicits more friendly interest, smiles and conversations than average, even from strangers. One report shows that 74 per cent of elderly people in one study felt better just by touching a pet!

Dogs provide a source of non-judgemental affection, and parents know that owning a pet can teach children responsibility. Dog ownership has been shown to boost self-esteem and even help develop a child's cognitive ability. Pets can also enhance family life through common affection for the animal.

So overwhelming is the evidence that pets are good for people that today they are being used for Animal-Assisted Therapy (AAT). Great stressbusters, pets are used to aid the recovery of people with long-term and even life-threatening illnesses. Lesley Scott Ordish, founder of the UK charity Pets As Therapy, set up the PAT Dogs scheme to enable elderly or ill people to experience the uplifting effects of contact with animals. PAT Dogs are ordinary dogs with placid temperaments whose owners take them into hospitals, nursing homes and hospices. Studies have shown that the recipients of pet visits, who may be depressed or seriously ill, smile more and become more responsive during and after the visits. If you think that your dog would make a good PAT dog and you are interested in becoming a regular hospital visitor, why not contact PAT Dogs (see page 127).

Health insurance for pets

It is possible to insure against the cost of veterinary treatment for dogs and cats, and many companies now offer a range of policies to suit the different needs of dog and cat owners. For an annual premium, most policies will guarantee to pay all your veterinary fees up to a maximum amount in each year. You will have to pay an agreed sum towards each claim. Some policies offer other kinds of cover as well. I fully recommend that you take out health insurance for your pet. Believe me, there is nothing worse than seeing owners distraught about their pet's illness or injury, and then having to cope with the additional worry of how they are going to pay for his expert care. You can't expect your vet centre to reduce its fees or to give you credit because you do not have sufficient available funds. Every vet centre is a business and must charge realistic fees to survive. When choosing which policy to take out, make sure that you read all the small print. If in doubt, consult an insurance advisor.

Policy details
A typical dog policy may cover the following:
- **Vet's fees for every illness and accident** – including any physiotherapy, acupuncture or herbal and homoeopathic medicines, hospitalisation and referral.
- **Death from illness or accident** – the cost of your dog (ie, what you paid when you bought him) reimbursed.
- **Boarding kennel fees** if you are taken into hospital for more than four days.
- **Holiday cancellation** – if your dog has emergency surgery up to seven days

Miss Button and Skippy have been inseparable companions ever since they met at the RSPCA centre at Great Ayton

before or whilst you are on holiday or goes missing while you are away.
- **Advertising and reward costs** – should your dog get lost or be stolen.
- **Loss by theft or straying** – the cost of your dog reimbursed.
- **Accidental damage** – caused by your dog to someone else's property.
- **Third party liability** – in case your dog causes damage or injury and you are legally liable.
- **Burglar reward** – if your dog catches an intruder in your home.

Annual premiums will vary and if you own a large breed of dog, you may have to pay a supplement. The pet health insurance market is a very competitive one and that's good news for pet owners. Companies are now much more imaginative about the kinds of cover they offer and are coming up with innovative ways of trying to reduce the costs. There are now policies designed specifically for families with more than one pet and some companies are offering no-claims discounts. So shop around.

From parrots to pigeons: encounters with feathered friends

MANY PEOPLE LOVE THE IDEA OF HAVING AN EXOTIC PARROT, SUCH AS AN AMAZON OR AFRICAN GREY AS A PET. LIKE ALL PARROTS, THEY ARE BEAUTIFUL CREATURES, AND, IF WELL CARED FOR, THEY BRING A LOT OF PLEASURE TO THEIR OWNERS. PARROTS ARE HIGHLY INTELLIGENT, SENSITIVE CREATURES THAT DESERVE A MUCH BETTER DEAL FROM US BOTH IN THE WILD AND IN CAPTIVITY. IN MY VIEW, KEEPING ANY KIND OF PET PARROT, EVEN A HUMBLE BUDGERIGAR, IS A MAJOR RESPONSIBILITY. ALL PARROT OWNERS MUST BE PREPARED TO ENSURE THAT THEIR BIRDS REMAIN BOTH PHYSICALLY FIT AND MENTALLY STIMULATED.

Sadly, many parrots are still caught from the wild, and suffer a terrifying and uncomfortable journey to their destination. Up to six out of ten of those caught are thought to die before they even leave their country of origin and more die on the journey. The Ministry of Agriculture estimates that around one in ten that make it here die in the first five weeks in the UK.

Far too many new owners take on parrots without understanding what sensitive, intelligent creatures they are. They do not provide for their physical and mental needs and the birds suffer terribly through neglect.

In February 1997, staff at RSPCA Great Ayton made a surprise discovery when Hartlepool CID arrested a pet-shop owner on a drugs-related matter. During questioning, the pet-shop owner handed over the keys to his shop so that detectives could conduct a thorough search of the premises. The police will not enter any premises where animals are kept without the presence of the RSPCA, and so Inspectors Derek Hall and Dave Fox were called to assist.

During their search for drugs they were surprised to find a number of

exotic birds locked away in a darkened room at the back of the shop. There was an extremely valuable blue-and-gold macaw, an African Grey parrot and three green Amazon parrots.

Because the birds were not being kept in the main part of the shop, Derek and Dave suspected that they were stolen. Amazingly, the birds appeared to be in good condition and had been kept in adequate cages, but there were no windows in the room, no light and dead mice lay scattered all about.

When the birds were brought to Great Ayton they were highly distressed. They squawked incessantly and their shrieks were deafening. Great Ayton's centre manager Maggie Eden described the birds upon their arrival at the centre as: 'Atrocious. They were extremely frightened and aggressive, and the noise they made was deafening. Because they were in OK condition there was no need for veterinary treatment so we just kept them in large individual cages and fed them a proprietary parrot mix and fresh food. Apart from that we tried to leave them alone as much as

Tracey Horrigan, an ambulance driver at Great Ayton, talks quietly to Sam, her African Grey parrot still traumatised from her life in darkness at a pet shop

possible in the hope that they would calm down. The minute anybody opened the door to the room in which they were kept, it sounded like there was a murder going on.'

Because the pet-shop owner co-operated fully and immediately signed the birds over to the care of the RSPCA, the Society decided not to pursue a prosecution case, and Maggie Eden thought it best not to try to determine the sexes of the birds as this would involve a surgical procedure that might further distress them in their already frightened state. As the days passed, the birds settled down and the noise levels abated somewhat, but they needed good homes.

Gradually, the new arrivals began to learn to trust humans. Inspector Jeff Edmunds took home one of the parrots and left the door of its cage open in the hope that it would slowly develop the confidence to venture outside. The parrot soon began to trust Jeff, and now takes peanuts from his hand.

Animal ambulance driver Tracey Horrigan has also adopted one of the birds, the African Grey, and reports similar experiences: 'She's brilliant, I love African Greys anyway, and she's a totally different bird from the one we brought home – much calmer and happier. We've called her Sam; we're guessing that she's female because she loves my husband so much and follows him everywhere! She's only ever in her cage at night and the rest of the time just wanders around the house. She's really settled in well and gets on great with our Rottweiler; in fact she was more scared of us than she was of the dog at first. The dog was curious to begin with, but now doesn't take much notice of her. They really seem to love each other.'

Parrots have no respect for interior furnishings and decor, but Tracey says that Sam hasn't been at all destructive. 'Her favourite spot is on the back of the settee, so we put a towel there to stop her picking at it. She's quite happy to sit there all the time and just watch what's going on. She's in wonderful shape. I've fostered other parrots before, and my favourite was an African Grey, which is why I chose Sam, but this is the first we've adopted – and we're delighted. She's wonderful.'

The other birds have also been successfully rehomed: the macaw now lives in the south of England and the remaining two parrots were rehomed together in a pub. The birds were clearly traumatised by their experiences, but with patient handling and correct husbandry they should enjoy long and happy lives.

A chicken-and-egg situation

When it comes to pet birds, the RSPCA doesn't just deal with parrot problems. One Monday in January 1997, RSPCA Great Ayton received an urgent call from a man whose father had died over the weekend, leaving some fifty ducks, thirty chickens, fifteen pigeons … oh yes, and about a dozen goldfish! All were urgently in need of care. His father had been extremely keen on poultry, but with his declining health the birds were a little neglected and were now in desperate need of adoption. The birds were kept in a series of sheds and hen-houses. The accommodation was spacious if a little dark, and because the birds were used to people they weren't too frightened, but they needed a new owner to take them on.

Inspectors Dave Fox, Derek Hall and Ian Jackson got the call to collect the birds. Ian said: 'You slightly dread a big job like this because you know you're going to be at it all day.' They went to get the birds, and had quite a job on their hands just figuring out which ones to catch and box up first.

The ducks were relatively docile and the pigeons didn't resist their capture too much. Nevertheless, it was one of those days that tests an RSPCA inspector's resolve and sense of humour. It was a miserable task, but not horrendous, according to Ian, 'if you don't mind being freezing cold, wet and covered in chicken shit'. The birds were put three to a box and then

When trying to place birds, RSPCA Great Ayton centre manager Maggie Eden has a list of regulars to contact

Steve Melalieu feeds his birds, which in turn provide him with eggs. They can wander freely during the day, and perch in the stables at night

loaded onto the vans to be transported back to Great Ayton. The fish were caught in nets and moved into a temporary holding tank for the journey.

Dave Fox was appalled by the smell of the duck house: 'You think you'd get used to it doing this job, but the smell is repulsive.' All the birds were a bit on the thin side and some had feather damage. All they needed was to be cared for and fed well for a few weeks before they were fit to be rehomed. The birds and fish all had a safe night in their new surroundings at Great Ayton, although they didn't show much interest in their food. The pigeons were moved to a large loft with plenty of room and light – an improvement on their previous surroundings, so it was hoped they would now be much happier.

The next day staff faced the task of finding new homes for such a large number of ducks and chickens. Their first step was to refer to the contact list that all RSPCA centres keep: this lists any people in the area that are interested in adopting certain animals. Centre manager Maggie Eden says: 'We have regulars on our list who we call up from time to time to take poultry, but we don't often have such a large number to rehome, so I was really asking big favours this time. Looking after such a large number of animals at the centre is a bit of a stretch on our time and resources, so I was keen to get them rehomed as quickly as possible.'

Steve Melalieu, who lives on the coast nine miles north of Whitby, was one of the first people she called. He came to have a look at the birds and chose eighteen hens and two ducks, bringing his total at home up to two dozen hens and six ducks. Steve is very interested in organically grown food and self-sufficiency and admits, 'The eggs are a bonus, but, best of all, the birds trim the weeds!' He also sells the eggs to friends and neighbours.

One of Steve Melalieu's twenty-four hens that help him weed his garden

Steve loves animals and also keeps guinea pigs and rabbits, which are fed some of the carrots he grows himself. The rescued birds now live in stables with nesting boxes and perches and seemed delighted with their new home. They wander freely during the day, but are kept in the stables at night. 'There were no problems with the new arrivals – the birds that were already here didn't take much notice, and they all just got on with it. I like keeping birds because they don't require an awful lot of maintenance and at least this way, I know where my eggs have come from. I'm very keen on eating organic produce and there's no surer way than to keep your own animals and grow your own vegetables.'

Meanwhile, Great Ayton staff have rehomed the remaining chickens in small groups to people who can prove they can raise them in a free-range environment. None of them will be used for commercial egg production.

Robson and Jerome: two dalmatian rabbits

WHENEVER I AM AT ONE OF THE RSPCA RESCUE CENTRES FEATURED IN *PET RESCUE*, I ALWAYS HAVE A WALK AROUND TO SEE WHO'S CHECKED OUT AND WHO'S CHECKED IN. EACH TIME I VISIT THERE ARE ONLY A FEW FAMILIAR FACES IN EITHER THE DOG KENNELS OR THE CATTERIES — A SURE SIGN THAT DOGS AND CATS ARE BEING REHOMED QUICKLY. BUT IT'S A VERY DIFFERENT STORY WHEN I POP IN ON THE RABBITS. MOST OF THEM I HAVE MET BEFORE, AND SOME OF THEM ARE NOW OLD FRIENDS. THEY ARE ALL WONDERFUL ANIMALS, AND EVERY ONE OF THEM DESPERATELY NEEDS AN OWNER WHO WILL BE COMMITTED TO NURTURING THEM AND BUILDING THEIR TRUST IN PEOPLE.

In my view rabbits are amongst the most neglected of Britain's pets. At any one time, around 500 rabbits are waiting to be rehomed in RSPCA centres around the country. The most common reason for their plight is simply this: they are bought by parents who mistakenly assume that the responsibility of caring for a rabbit will be good for their children. Once the novelty has worn off, the children lose interest, and the unwanted rabbits are brought to animal rescue centres all over the country. Worse still, every year hundreds of rabbits are abandoned in city centres or on roadsides and left to their fate.

The subject of *Pet Rescue's* TV Easter Special in spring 1997 was to try to rehome as many as possible of the rabbits living at RSPCA rescue centres all over Britain. Because of the popularity of the series, everyone involved had high hopes that many rabbits would find homes — the *Pet Rescue* appeal line gets hundreds of calls every day, and you can read about how the appeals are organised later in this chapter, on page 60. Four rabbits, one with a litter of kittens, were featured on this appeal, and three of them were rehomed. In total, ten days after the appeal, over 800 rabbits had been found good new homes.

Two dalmatian rabbits with spectacular black-and-white markings were featured in one of our very first appeals. Brothers Robson and Jerome were part of an unwanted litter of rabbit kittens a few months old. They arrived at RSPCA Millbrook in Chobham in January 1997. Shortly after their appeal was broadcast, there was a set-back. The two seemed to have a falling out. Both adolescent males, they had begun, quite naturally, to fight. So the staff at Millbrook arranged for them both to be neutered. In many cases this helps to reduce or eliminate aggression and in their case it worked a treat. After the operations they were soon best buddies.

There was a tremendous response to the appeal for a home for them. Some 597 people offered to adopt Robson and Jerome. The successful applicants were the Groombridge family of Chessington in Surrey. Shortly before Christmas their eight-year-old son Jason had been devastated when his cat Scrappy was run over by a car. The Groombridges were desperate to get another pet for their son, but keen to avoid another cat that might run into the road just as Scrappy had. When Joyce Groombridge saw the *Pet Rescue* appeal, she thought that rabbits might make the ideal pets for Jason. The Groombridges had always kept rabbits in the family when their daughters were growing up, and so were familiar with their special needs.

Every day Jason brings both rabbits indoors after school and plays with them indoors for a couple of hours. He loves his new pets, and this kind of regular handling will help to keep them tame and accustomed to human contact. Unless rabbits are handled regularly they can quickly revert to their natural instincts, which are to bolt very quickly and to fear people. Both Robson and Jerome are extremely affectionate and love to hop around the house when they are brought inside. Perhaps one day they may move inside full time. It's not out of the question because rabbits can be toilet-trained! (See more on pages 58 and 59.)

There are two million rabbits living as domestic pets in the UK. Many lead lonely, inactive lives, neglected in hutches at the bottom of people's gardens. But Robson and Jerome are in clover in their new home. Joyce says that the family are 'delighted with Robson and Jerome. They seem to be settling in very well'.

Gradually, the family began to notice Robson and Jerome's individual characters emerging. Jerome is nosy and mischievous (he has chewed through the telephone wire and got himself stuck behind the piano – if you have rabbits indoors, you need to supervise them closely), whereas Robson is a more serious, reserved chap. They will both come up to every member of the family for a stroke and cuddle! Each morning before school Jason lets them out of their enclosure so they can have a run around the garden.

'They're cutting the lawn nicely,' says Joyce. Jason is now responsible for Robson and Jerome, and gets their food from the pet shop. He also makes fresh food for them: little bits of cabbage and carrots are their favourites.

Setting up home properly for rabbits can be quite expensive – expect to pay £80 to £100 for good-sized living accommodation plus more for suitable fencing for the obligatory enclosure. But Joyce reckons that it costs less than £1 per month to feed both rabbits, the only other investment being their straw, and, of course, their routine veterinary care – rabbits need vaccinating every year.

Rabbits as indoor pets

For me, one of the most exciting recent developments in the world of pet care is the new but growing trend of keeping rabbits as indoor rather than outdoor pets. When caring for any animal, an owner's responsibility is not only to keep their pet alive, but to make sure that he stays both physically and mentally fit.

I cannot believe that people who keep rabbits in small hutches, only letting them out for a few minutes once a day for a cuddle – something that the rabbit probably finds quite frightening because they are handled so little – don't care about them. I am sure that, in fact, quite the opposite is true. It's just that few owners in my experience really understand the animals that they are trying to care for. They assume that rabbits are simple animals with simple needs. Well, nothing could be further from the truth.

In many ways, pet rabbits are very different from their wild cousins, but they also share much in common, particularly in relation to their behaviour. Wild rabbits are social creatures, but they do not like company forced upon them in cramped accommodation. They are naturally very timid animals that spend their lives assuming that at any moment they will have to run for their lives – with eyes on the sides of their heads and huge ears, they are well geared up for the early detection of potential predators ... including people!

So, to gain an insight into the kinds of things pet rabbits might like to do in a day and the amount of time they may like to spend doing those things, it is worth taking a look at their wild side. One group of well-studied wild rabbits were shown to spend sixteen hours a day in their burrows and eight hours out and about. Of that eight hours they occupied their time as follows:

- **Feeding** – 4 hours and 24 minutes
- **Resting** – 38 minutes
- **Looking around** – 1 hour and 36 minutes
- **Moving about** – 24 minutes
- **Grooming** – 22 minutes
- **Scent-marking objects** – 6 minutes
- **Scraping at ground** – 7 minutes
- **Sniffing ground** – 12 minutes
- **Active courtship** – 7 minutes
- **Active aggression** – 4 minutes

Claudia at RSPCA Millbrook with Jerome before he was rehomed. All rabbits need handling regularly to keep them tame

All rabbits are naturally shy of people. To win Robson and Jerome's trust, Jason Groombridge began by feeding them favourite foods from outside their enclosure

One main responsibility of rabbit ownership is providing the opportunity for them to behave naturally (except for courtship, of course!). Be honest – how many pet rabbits do you know that are allowed out of their hutches for eight hours a day?

The reason I am so excited about the evolving craze of keeping them indoors as house pets is that I think rabbit owners will grow to understand their pets better and will be much more committed to offering them the kind of lifestyle they deserve if they and their rabbits are living together rather than apart. At the end of the garden it is all too easy for rabbits to be out of sight and out of mind.

If you decide to house-train your rabbit, he will still need to run outside every day – under your supervision if you don't have a pen for him to exercise in. On the next two pages are some of the things you will need to consider if you decide to house-train your rabbit. Remember that there is no one right way to do it, but the following points are a guide.

For more information contact the British House Rabbit Association (address on page 126).

It is easiest to train young rabbits under six months old. An older rabbit that has been spending a lot of time alone in a hutch at the bottom of the garden may prove more difficult to train.

Before you take your rabbit to live inside you will need to make sure your home is safe enough. Rabbits are natural gnawers, so make sure they can't get at electric flexes. Hide mains wires under the floor or carpet. You can protect TV aerial and speaker cables with plastic piping. Put objects that a rabbit cannot move in front of plug sockets. Some house plants may be poisonous to him, so check with your vet if you're not sure which ones are safe.

The next step is to set up a 'home' for your rabbit indoors, and to teach him to use a litter tray. You will need a puppy pen or a large cage as a den with a hay-lined box inside for sleeping in. Your rabbit will need clean water every day as well as dried and fresh food and his home should be somewhere quiet, away from other pets. Part of the pen should be covered, to give him a feeling of security.

Put a litter tray in a dark, private part of his home. Rabbits are clean animals and naturally use the same spot for their toilet again and again. To begin with, introduce a litter tray to his hutch so he can get used to it in familiar surroundings. Fill it with lightly soiled litter, so that his scent is strong in the new tray. When he is using it in his hutch, you can move him and the tray indoors. Again, when you are sure that he is using the tray in his den, you can start to let him out for about ten minutes twice a day. Entice him back in with a treat, such as a carrot. Once he is returning to his pen without problems and is using the litter tray inside the pen, you can begin to let him out for longer periods.

Make sure you supervise him all the time. After about a month he should be trained as a house rabbit. Many rabbits can then be left to wander the house at will, though some will always need a watchful eye. Unlike a dog or cat he will want to spend a lot of time in his own area, and you can keep him amused by giving him cardboard boxes and newspaper to chew up.

When he is out of his pen it is a good idea to offer him a choice of litter-tray locations just in case he wants to go to the toilet but feels for some reason that his route back to his pen is temporarily blocked. To begin with, place some lightly soiled litter from his main tray in any other trays, so that he recognises what they are for.

Rabbits will naturally want to gnaw at novel objects, possibly even your best furniture, but you can train them to stop doing it. When they start chewing at furniture say 'NO' in a loud voice, or stamp your foot on the floor – rabbits drum their back feet on the ground as a warning to each other. If he persists, a short, sharp squirt from a well-aimed water-pistol can be useful. Make sure he can't see that you're spraying him (difficult as he can see all around him) or he will fear you and your relationship will deteriorate. If he latches on to the fact that every time he starts chewing he gets a dousing, he's much more likely to stop.

At other times, try to keep reasonably quiet around him – don't shout or run around (the vibrations might upset him), and keep him in his pen when you're using the vacuum cleaner, as he will probably be frightened by the noise.

Pet Rescue appeals

The first step in setting up the appeals that come at the end of *Pet Rescue* every weekday was to ask all the RSPCA and SSPCA (Scottish Society for the Prevention of Cruelty to Animals) centres which of them wanted to take part. Most centres said they did, so Tracy Edwards, *Pet Rescue's* Appeals Director, found out how large each centre was and what sort of animals could be cared for there. The centres vary greatly in size, and some have facilities only for smaller animals, while others can take larger animals such as horses.

To choose the five appeals for the week, Tracy selects five centres spread all over the country, and phones them to ask them for their most suitable candidates for rehoming. She makes sure that, as well as a good geographical spread, there is a variety of animals – say two dogs, a cat, a larger animal like a pony, and a smaller animal, such as a gerbil or guinea pig. Often the appeals feature dogs that have been kennelled for a long time and are having trouble attracting a new owner, or cruelty cases.

When the appeal is broadcast, people interested in adopting an animal telephone the appeal hotline. Callers, who must be over eighteen to adopt an animal, leave their contact details on an answerphone. These details are processed overnight and passed to the RSPCA. Most of the appeals receive 200 to 300 calls, but a few have attracted at least double that. The RSPCA prefers to home the animal near the centre that is running the appeal, so that they can do a home-check (see page 122). All the callers in the local area are contacted by the RSPCA centre in question, while people that have phoned from other parts of the country are replied to by letter and contacted by their local RSPCA office to find out if they are interested in adopting another aniimal.

When a suitable new owner is found, they come to meet the animal, and a home-check visit is carried out. Finally, the animal is vaccinated and neutered (unless this has already been done or is contrary to veterinary advice), the paperwork is completed, and they go off together to a happy new life. New owners may have to pay a fee for adopting a pet – up to £40 for a cat and up to £100 for a pedigree dog. But these fees vary from centre to centre.

One of the additional benefits of the appeals has been to alert people to the fact that there are animal rescue centres all over the country, and they have raised awareness of the huge variety of animals cared for by them. The appeals often generate interest in particular centres, so that animals who are not part of the appeal are also rehomed.

Rocky: a stressed dog finally finds a loving home

RSPCA CENTRES ARE VERY BUSY PLACES, AND ONE OF THE BIGGEST CHORES IS CLEANING THE DOG KENNELS, AS I DISCOVERED FIRST HAND WHEN I OFFERED TO HELP OUT ONE DAY. WORKING INSIDE THE KENNELS, THE ONE THING THAT REALLY HIT ME WAS HOW LONELY I FELT. I DON'T THINK IT IS TOO FAR FETCHED TO BELIEVE THAT MANY DOGS FEEL THE SAME WAY WHEN THEY ARE CONFINED. KENNEL DESIGN AND THE WAY DOGS ARE CARED FOR IN THEM IS A VERY SERIOUS ISSUE THAT IS NOW RECEIVING THE ATTENTION OF VETS AND OTHER ANIMAL WELFARE EXPERTS. IT IS NOW GENERALLY ACCEPTED THAT TRADITIONAL DOG KENNELS ARE FAR FROM IDEAL – THEY WERE ORIGINALLY DESIGNED WITH EASE OF CLEANING IN MIND. BUT, HOPEFULLY, IN THE FUTURE A BIGGER PRIORITY WILL BE THE NEEDS OF THE DOGS WHO ARE EXPECTED TO LIVE IN THEM.

Dogs are intelligent, social creatures that in general do not cope well with isolation. The RSPCA knows only too well that some dogs confined to kennels become anxious and agitated. They cannot settle, and indulge in repetitive behaviour patterns such as pacing, jumping and circling. Their behaviour is often referred to as kennel stress. Some of the symptoms of kennel stress, such as jumping, may begin as the dog attempts to see other dogs that it can only hear. Other behaviours such as circling are more difficult to interpret. One suggestion is that by indulging in repetitive behaviours kennel-stressed dogs may benefit from the effects of released body chemicals called endorphins, which create a feeling of well being and so may help them cope with their feelings of anxiety at being confined.

Rocky, a five-year-old tan-and-white mongrel, came to RSPCA Bradford when his owner died. He lived in kennels there for seven months before being transferred to RSPCA Millbrook. Rocky had developed typical symptoms of kennel stress, and would-be owners simply passed him by, labelling him a neurotic dog – something he most certainly is not. The Bradford centre were finding it difficult to rehome him, and it was hoped that Millbrook would have more luck. Sue Walters, Millbrook's deputy manager, says, 'He's a sweet dog with a lovely nature who developed these problems through no fault of his own. It's sad and all too common for dogs that are kennelled for any length of time, I'm afraid.'

Rocky's eccentric-seeming behaviour was reducing his chances of being rehomed. Animal behaviourist Rebecca Ledger describes this as a 'common Catch-22 situation. They desperately need new homes to solve their problems, but precisely because of these problems they are unlikely to appeal to a new owner. Meanwhile, the poor dog is having to work hard physically to cope with the psychological pressures of his environment. It's very distressing for the animal, and painful to watch.'

To make matters worse, Rocky was barking at other dogs, and, when people came to see him, he would jump up at them, so Sue Walters decided to try to 'disc-train' him as a way of helping to gain more control over his unwanted behaviour (you can read more about disc training on page 67). Unless he was controllable in the presence of would-be owners it would be unlikely that anyone would want to take him on. She also made sure that he got taken out for walks more often to help reduce his boredom, and gave him interesting toys to play with. I suggested filling a strong rubber hollow toy with food. It's a simple way of occupying a dog's time in very natural behaviour. Trying to get the food out of the toy is like trying to get marrow out of a bone. It can keep some dogs occupied for quite long periods. The more time Rocky was occupied, the less likely he would be to pace, jump and circle.

It all seemed to help and, before too long, Chris and Gerry Samuel-Camps from Aldershot visited Millbrook in search of a new dog and took a shine to Rocky. When they took him for a walk, they really liked his enthusiastic temperament and thought he seemed very well behaved, but they were concerned about how well Rocky would get on with their two young children.

Centre manager Tony Glue suggested that they bring the children to visit Rocky and play with him at Millbrook. During the visit Rocky was at first distracted by the tantalising sight of George, the centre's cat, patrolling on the other side of the compound fence, but with attention from the entire Samuel-Camps family, soon began to respond very well. When the children stroked Rocky, he wagged his tail with delight and, more importantly, kept all four feet on the ground.

The matter was decided then and there, and once the paperwork was completed Rocky climbed excitedly into the car for the journey back to his new home.

For the first couple of days Rocky was a little excitable, but as he became accustomed to his new-found freedom in a loving environment, he settled down brilliantly. 'To be perfectly honest, nothing was said to us about Rocky suffering from kennel stress, so we weren't sure what the bouncing up and down was all about. It was only later that we were told about his condition. I don't think, ultimately, it would have put us off had we known from the beginning, but it might have given us pause for thought. There were no problems with the children, so we assumed that he was fine.'

Rocky adores the children and is very affectionate with strangers. He was rather curious about the family's two canaries, and liked to sit and watch them a lot. But he doesn't seem interested in their fish! The family does not anticipate any problems, because Rocky is friendly towards other dogs, and not at all aggressive towards anything or anyone.

Rocky's story is a good indication of just how quickly so-called 'problem dogs' with kennel stress can adapt to a new home, even after months of confinement, given the right kind of care.

Is your dog getting the most out of life?

The quality of your dog's life is more important to him than the quantity of it. After all, he does not worry about the future. Like all dogs, he focuses on the present. For him, life is lived day by day.

In the wild, a wolf (your dog's wild ancestor) leads an unpredictable kind of lifestyle. For him, there is no guarantee of a warm bed and a nourishing meal each and every day. He is constantly stressed and stimulated by the world he lives in. Sudden changes in the weather, rivalry with other wolves and the inherent dangers of long and exhausting hunting expeditions are just some of the things that he has to cope with. But his body and brain are well suited for it. Pet dogs, on the other hand, often lead very predictable lives. Many owners feel the need to protect them as if they are helpless babies, even when their dogs are fully grown adults. Of course, some kinds of pet dog require a great deal of cosseting because the size, shape and structure of their bodies is so far removed from what would

Chocolate Chip makes mischief at Milbrook

Bambi at
home in
Esher, Surrey

Duchess
with owner
Jill Dean

Star-crossed lovers Loxley and Rainbow

Rainbow on
the Yorkshire
Moors

Miss Button
with Skippy

Sam, the
African Grey
Parrot

Two of Steve
Melalieu's
ducks

Jerome before
he was
rehomed

Rocky plays
at home

Wild swan at
Billingham
Beck Valley
Country Park

Big Fella
enjoys life at
Proteus

Jensen with Neil McGuiness

Peggy in Catherine Moore's garden

John and
friends at
Scarborough's
seal hospital

*Rocky plays with
Jenny and Paul
Samuel-Camps.
Rocky wagged his
tail with delight
when he first met
the family*

be required for them to survive in the wild on their own. And who knows what domestication has really done to their brains?

But, even if your dog is a Pekinese, don't just assume that he wants to be waited on hand and foot. Try to expose your dog to new and stimulating experiences. Don't go on the same walk at the same time every day. Train him properly so that you can let him off the lead when you are out and about. Some dogs are never let free to roam and explore when out exercising because their owners are convinced that they won't come back. What a shame for those dogs. How they must long to flare their nostrils and get some wind through their hair. Variety is the spice of life.

There is more to play than simply throwing a rubber ball for him to fetch, but your dog will enjoy some experiences more than others. He may think that a new game that you have come up with is dull and he may just walk away as soon as you start playing it. That's great. He had the choice, and he decided to say no. If it is cold and raining and you would normally take your dog out for a walk but he really does not want to go, don't force him. It is not obligatory to exercise any dog for a precise number of minutes every day.

The amount of exercise that a dog needs to stay fit relates to the kind of lifestyle he leads. Some dogs may get adequate physical exercise just pottering around a large garden. But that doesn't mean that these dogs shouldn't go for walks. The whole point of exercising your dog is not only to physically exert him but also to stimulate his mind. A dog that is taken for very regular but very boring walks may be no more physically fit than a dog that has exciting and interesting walks less frequently, supplemented by lots of games and play at home. But mentally he will be much worse off.

Your personal circumstances, interests and abilities will influence the kind of lifestyle that you give your dog. So think carefully if you're in the process of choosing a canine companion. You may be able to offer a Cavalier King Charles spaniel quality of life, but would struggle to mentally and physically entertain some kinds of terrier of a similar size.

Be prepared to break with tradition and dare to be a different kind of dog owner. Plan a full, varied and fun life for your dog. By feeding your dog a good diet, giving him somewhere to rest his head and taking him for two walks around the block every day you will be able to keep him physically healthy enough. But if that's all there is to his life, will he be truly happy? Would he rather swap one of the walks for a fun game with an interesting toy at home in your back garden? Perhaps in the long term more interesting walks less frequently would suit him better.

Experiment with his lifestyle. When appropriate and as often as possible, give him the freedom to make a few decisions for himself. Most of us would agree that by far the worst thing about pet dogs is that they don't live long enough. It's up to you to make sure he gets the most out of his relatively short life.

You not only decide most of what your dog does, but you also decide when he does it. Exercise and play is the one area of his life where he can and should make some decisions for himself. So, give him the freedom to choose the kinds of activities that he finds most stimulating. Provide him with plenty of options.

There are only three essential things for you to bear in mind – variety, variety and variety!

Remember that different breeds like different activites, but a few things you can try for variety are:

• **Walks on the lead** – These will accustom your dog to traffic. Hard surfaces such as pavements will help keep his nails in good condition, too.

• **Walks off the lead** – You need to be confident that he'll come back when called, and make sure you're in control of him at gates and other obstacles, especially if he's young, as he may try something dangerously acrobatic.

• **Swimming** – Make sure the water is fairly clean and not fast flowing, and check to see that there's an easy exit before letting him jump in.

• **Games** – 'Fetch' is a real favourite, as is 'find my owner'. If you play tug of war, make sure you start and end the game, and train your dog to drop the object on command. Offer toys in rotation to maintain your dog's interest.

Disc training

Discing is a special training method which was invented by animal behaviourist John Fisher. It allows dog owners to control their dog's unwanted behaviour through the unique sound of 'chinking' a set of small brass discs. The dog is trained by a special technique to learn that the sound of the discs means that his behaviour will not be rewarded, but that if he immediately focuses his attention on his owner, he will be rewarded. The discs are not used to frighten or alarm the dog.

In the wild, dogs are pack animals, and the pack will always have a leader. Before you can start training your dog, make sure he knows you're the pack leader. You don't need to use aggression or confrontation to do this, but gently reinforce your position in a number of ways. For example: don't let your dog go through a doorway or down a corridor in front of you; don't let him onto beds or chairs. Most important of all, it is essential that your dog responds to basic commands, such as 'sit'.

Two of Rocky's 'problems' were that he barked at other dogs and jumped up at people, and Sue used the discs to help train him out of these habits. Once Rocky had learned the meaning of the sound of the discs, Sue progressed on to using them to control these 'bad habits'. 'Once Rocky was keyed into the sound of the discs, I could teach him not to jump up and bark so much.' The Samuel-Camps family carried on training him in the same way once they took him home.

Waterfowl: innocents in a modern world

IN THE WILD, LIFE FOR ANY ANIMAL IS A CONSTANT STRUGGLE, AND IS MADE SO MUCH MORE DIFFICULT BY THE MANY MAN-MADE HAZARDS WE PUT IN THEIR WAY. IT'S UNPALATABLE, I KNOW, BUT WE HAVE TO FACE UP TO THE FACT THAT OUR ACTIVITIES RESULT IN THE DEATH OR INJURY OF MILLIONS OF WILD MAMMALS, BIRDS, REPTILES AND FISH EVERY YEAR. I OFTEN VISIT WILDLIFE HOSPITALS AND RESCUE CENTRES AND ALWAYS LEAVE FEELING EMBARRASSED TO BE HUMAN. SO MANY OF THE PATIENTS THAT I SEE ARE ONLY THERE BECAUSE THEIR LIVES AND OURS HAVE CLASHED HEAD ON. WITH A LITTLE THOUGHT WE CAN ALL DO MORE TO HELP PREVENT WILDLIFE CASUALTIES.

Disposing of our litter carefully is just one way. Plastic binding of the kind that holds together beer and soft drink cans causes untold damage: it can entangle an animal or be swallowed with deadly consequences. Bottles can be death traps for small animals such as mice and voles, who can't get out once they get in, and tins and yoghurt pots are dangerous for animals like hedgehogs, which can get their heads stuck in them when they investigate the smell of food.

Caring for and treating wild animals that are ill or injured should most definitely be left to the experts. It's all too easy for untrained, inexperienced hands to do more harm than good. Every year the RSPCA helps thousands of pet animals back to health after humans have neglected them, or injured them either accidentally or deliberately. But it also helps many wild animals.

The RSPCA has found that discarded fishing tackle – lines, hooks and nets – is often the cause of injury and death in wild animals, especially bird life. In 1995 the RSPCA carried out a survey that showed that swans (including many cygnets), coots, ducks, geese, gulls and moorhens were the worst affected. Over a six-month period, RSPCA inspectors spent around 200 working days dealing with the consequences of litter on or near water in England and Wales, and were called to help well over a thousand animals affected by fishing litter.

Lines can wrap round an animal and cut off blood supply to parts of its body. Hooks and weights can be swallowed, get stuck and cause internal blockage, injury or death. Swallowed lead weights cause lead poisoning. Nets can trap animals, leaving them with no means of escape.

In October 1996 RSPCA Great Ayton received a call from Howard Ward, a warden at Billingham Beck Valley Country Park near Middlesbrough, who reported a sighting of a swan that had flown into another man-made hazard, an electric pylon.

The swan was one of Britain's commonest breeds, the mute swan (see page 70 for tips on how to identify swans in Britain). Although swans are extremely strong flyers – the whooper and Bewick's swans migrate as far as Siberia and back in a year – they lack manoeuvrability. The swan may well have seen the pylon, but probably too late to avoid it.

Howard found the swan on one of Billingham Beck Valley's ponds with blood coming from its neck. It looked lethargic and unwell. Its partner was staying close and loyally protecting it, although Howard is convinced that both swans were male! RSPCA Inspector Ian Jackson was despatched to try to catch the bird with a swan hook, a long pole with a loop on the end for placing over the swan's head and around the neck. The idea was to capture the swan and bring it to Great Ayton for medical attention.

But the injured swan proved evasive and despite Ian Jackson's best attempts, it managed to avoid its would-be captor. Ian says, 'I tried it from all angles, all sides of the pond. The minute I went to one side of the pond, it moved to the other. We carried on this cat-and-mouse game for a couple of hours, but by this time he knew that I was after him and he was determined not to be caught. I tried lying very low and pretending to ignore the swan, but he was too smart for that and eventually I had to admit defeat.'

Despite an afternoon's strenuous work trying to lure it, the swan evaded capture and eventually grew so suspicious that it wouldn't even come near the banks of the pond. The RSPCA and Billingham Beck Valley's wardens kept an eye on it over the course of a few weeks. Fortunately, the swan's wound seemed to heal naturally and now it and its partner have moved on.

Owen Wilson, who also works as a warden at Billingham Beck Valley, explained that the mute swan's case was very unusual. 'Pylons have never been a major threat here to swans because the electricity board places markers on the lines. However, the swans are more often disturbed by dogs, and are also sometimes attacked by people with airguns,' he says.

Thankfully, most of the birds at Billingham Beck Valley, which include herons, moorhens, coots, kingfishers and partridges, are well protected in the park's 120 acres, but as our story shows, anything can happen.

What to do if you see injured waterfowl

Tim Thomas from the RSPCA's Wildlife Department has this to say on finding an injured bird, or indeed any wild animal that you think is hurt: 'The best advice is to simply leave it alone. Too many people fancy themselves as animal doctors and this often causes more damage than the original injury. Wherever you are in the UK, there will be an animal rescue centre nearby and your first duty is to call them and wait for expert care.

'If you really want to be of help, just stand by and monitor the situation and note anything the animal does – this kind of information may be useful to the inspector when he or she arrives. I cannot stress enough that you should let these animals be and leave their care to an expert. I don't think people mean to hurt the animals – indeed, they are usually trying to help – but an injured animal in receipt of amateur care is in far greater danger than one just left alone until expert help arrives.'

How to recognise swans in the British Isles

The mute swan is Britain's commonest swan, and can be found all year round nearly everywhere in the British Isles, except for the very far north of Scotland. It has white feathers and an orange bill, with a black knob at the base of the bill. Adult males have long, curved necks, and a larger knob on their bills than females. As they fly, their wing beats make a humming or buzzing noise.

Interestingly, all mute swans on the Thames are owned by the Queen or one of two London livery companies, the Vintner's and the Dyer's Company.

The whooper swan and Bewick's swan are very similar in appearance, and they both visit the British Isles between October and April. Bewick's swans are seen on the south coast as well as other coastal regions, but the whooper swan prefers northern parts. They both have white feathers and yellow bills tipped with black, and fly almost silently. The main differences between them are:
• The whooper swan is named for its loud call, and is larger than Bewick's swan. It also has a more angular yellow patch on its bill, and a longer neck.
• Bewick's swan honks rather than trumpeting like the whooper swan. It has a more rounded head, a smaller yellow patch on its bill and a shorter neck. In flight it looks quite goose-like.

A mute swan at Billingham Beck Valley Country Park

Two geese at RSPCA Great Ayton. One of the most common hazards for wildfowl is discarded fishing litter, such as hooks, nets and lines

Litter can injure or kill animals

Dispose of your litter carefully: a little thought can save lives. The RSPCA recommends that you:

• **Tie a knot** in all plastic bags before throwing them away, as animals are less likely to be able to climb inside them. Re-use plastic carrier bags as many times as you can, or take them to your local recycling centre.

• **Take cans** to your recycling centre, or, if you have to throw them away, remove the lid completely and drop it to the bottom of the can. Pinch the top shut so that small animals can't climb in, and larger ones can't get their heads stuck.

• **Remove the lids** completely from yoghurt pots and scrunch the lids up. This reduces the chances of an animal getting its head stuck inside the pot.

• **Cut up rubber bands** and the loops that hold drink cans together before throwing them away.

• **Take all bottles and jars** to your recycling centre. If you can't recycle plastic bottles, cut them in half before throwing them out, so that small animals can't get trapped inside.

• **Put unwanted fishing tackle** in a bag and then in a bin, or take it home with you. Destroy unwanted fishing line by cutting it into small lengths or burning it. Never leave baited fishing tackle unattended.

• **Do not tip solvents or sump oil** down the drain. Your local garage or council may have an oil collection point. If you see anyone dumping these substances, or any signs of pollution, call the Environment Agency on 0800 807060.

Big Fella: the victim of a cartoon craze

MY EXPERIENCE AND THAT OF OTHERS INVOLVED IN REPTILE RESCUE SUGGESTS THAT PEOPLE TYPICALLY TAKE ON EXOTIC ANIMALS LIKE SNAKES, LIZARDS AND TURTLES WITHOUT ANY UNDERSTANDING OF HOW TO CARE FOR THEM PROPERLY. REPTILES ARE VERY COMPLEX ANIMALS WITH INCREDIBLY SPECIAL NEEDS. PROTEUS REPTILE RESCUE IN BIRMINGHAM IS THE ONLY REPTILE RESCUE CENTRE IN THE UK REGULARLY USED BY THE RSPCA. ITS HEADQUARTERS IS CONSTANTLY FULL OF UNWANTED, ADANDONED AND ABUSED REPTILES, AND IT HAS A WAITING LIST OF PEOPLE WHO WANT TO OFFLOAD THEIR EXOTIC PETS. THE VOLUNTEERS WHO WORK THERE SIMPLY DO THE BEST THEY CAN TO PICK UP THE PIECES WHEN AGAIN AND AGAIN THE REPTILE OWNERSHIP DREAM TURNS TO REAL-LIFE NIGHTMARE.

The unassuming red-eared terrapin must be the world's most commonly abandoned pet reptile. This appealing little creature was thrust into the limelight with the enormous commercial success of the Teenage Mutant Ninja Turtle cartoon characters in the early 1990s. A terrapin-buying craze was on, but with scant information available, thousands of terrapins bought by ill-informed owners were doomed to miserable, short lives.

Peter Heathcote, founder and trustee of Proteus Reptile Rescue, says, '$19 billion was made in the USA from the sale of red-eared terrapins, but 99 per cent of the terrapins sold died before they were six months old. The Teenage Mutant Ninja Turtles are the main cause of the terrapin problem we have in Britain. The craze has slowed down, but we are dealing with the aftermath.'

Red-eared terrapins, which are bred in the USA, flooded pet shops in the UK, but many pet-shop owners were unable to provide potential terrapin owners with pet-care advice. Big Fella was no exception. Brought into RSPCA Great Ayton in November 1996, she had grown much larger than her owner had expected. At about a month old Big Fella was only the size of a fifty-pence piece, but within the space of a few months had outgrown the size of the tiny glass tank she was forced to live in. Her owner – who had thought Big Fella was a male, hence her name – decided she couldn't care for her bigger-than-expected terrapin, so Great Ayton staff set about making her more comfortable. She was trying to climb out of her small aquarium and rolling onto her back, but was soon rehoused in a larger temporary tank.

When I visited Great Ayton the first thing I noticed was that Big Fella's name didn't match her sex! The way to sex a terrapin is to look at the claws. The males have extremely long nails compared with the females. Also the tail of the male is a lot wider and longer than that of the female.

Several weeks later Big Fella was joined by another terrapin, and together they were transferred to Proteus Reptile Rescue. Big Fella and her new friend were collected from Great Ayton in one of Proteus's two special reptile ambulances, and from there made their long journey to Birmingham.

Peter Heathcote, who is a herpetologist (reptile specialist) says Big Fella had recovered from her initial distress, and soon settled in well at Proteus. 'She was in fairly good shape by the time we got her. Putting her in a bigger tank had helped. She was probably trying to escape her tiny tank to lay eggs – terrapins lay unfertilised eggs just like chickens do,' he says.

Peter says that many people buy reptiles on impulse with little thought for their needs. 'They are novelty pets who suffer through the ignorance of their owners. Terrapins, which need warm water to survive, are even sold as cold-water animals. Buyers often have no concept of the size terrapins grow to, or how long they can live for.'

We are well informed as to the needs of dogs and cats, but when it comes to reptiles, we have little conception of how to care for them properly. Often, people find that looking after terrapins is too much like hard work, and they are frequently dumped into rivers and streams where they can die slow and agonising deaths. The weather and water temperature in Britain is simply too cold for them. In the first year of being released into a pond or river they lose body fat and in the second year are likely to develop pneumonia and gradually die.

Could you care for a terrapin?

Like all reptiles, terrapins have very special needs, and to care for them properly owners must be prepared to invest in necessary technology.

• **Ultra-violet light** – Terrapins need ultra-violet light to synthesise vitamin D3 to keep their shells strong. If they do not get it they suffer from a condition known as soft shell, and can die. In the wild, direct sunlight provides them with

UVB (a type of ultra-violet light), but the sun's UV rays will not penetrate glass, so you can't leave a tank near the window hoping that the sun will provide for your terrapin's UV needs. You should buy a UVB tube specially designed for reptiles: other types of ultra-violet lights will not do. This light should be left on for up to fourteen hours a day and will need replacing every six months.

• **A basking lamp** – Because terrapins are 'cold blooded', they raise their body temperature by basking in the sun. At home you can simulate their natural habitat by setting up a 40–60 watt reflector lamp above a rock or basking area. The temperature on the rock needs to be around 29°C (84°F) so put a thermometer on the rock and adjust the height of the bulb until the right temperature is reached. Leave the light on all day, but turn it off at night. The sun doesn't shine at night!

• **A water heater** – Terrapins cannot thrive in cold water. The water should remain at a constant temperature of about 22–24°C (72–75°F), day and night, a little lower than the air temperature terrapins need. This will encourage your terrapin to leave the water to bask and therefore reduce the risk of shell problems.

• **A water filter** – This makes sure the tank water is kept free of debris. It will need cleaning every day. You will also need to change the tank water regularly, but make sure the clean water is warm enough.

By the way, terrapins like to wander around the garden or living room, although a watchful eye is necessary. They can move faster than you think!

Red-eared terrapin fact file

• **The word terrapin** derives from the American Indian word for 'little turtle'.
• **The red-eared terrapin** or red-eared slider, as it is often called, is the most common pet terrapin. Its scientific name is *Trachemys scripta elegans*. They are called sliders because of their habit of scurrying into the water when frightened. They are also referred to as the elegant terrapin.
• **They can be found** in the wild from eastern USA southwards into Mexico.
• **The terrapin is farmed** both in North America and in Malaysia for the pet market, but according to Proteus, the vast majority die soon after arrival in the UK.
• **Individuals from northern states** are better adapted to our cooler climate than those from warmer areas, but they look identical.
• **Size** – They grow up to 30 cm (12 inches) long. Initial growth is fast.
• **Age** – They may live for up to forty years. Some are said to have lived to be 100!
• **Sex** – Males are smaller than females and have much longer front claws. In the UK there tend to be more females than males, as farms have

*Big Fella was
only the size of a
fifty-pence piece
when her owner
bought her, but
she was the size
of a side-plate
when she was
rescued*

artificially high temperatures in order to increase productivity and this results in more females hatching than males.

Basic housing needs

• **Space** – Opinions on this vary, but I recommend a rectangular aquarium or indoor pond. You need at least 1 square metre of space for a terrapin 10cm long, 2 square metres for a terrapin 20cm long, and so on.

• **They must have a haul-out area** as they spend a considerable amount of time basking on land.

• **Two areas of land must be supplied** – One away from the heat/light source and the other directly under it.

• **The land can be rocks** but cork bark works well as it floats.

• **They must have good ventilation**

• **The water does not need to be deep all over** – It's better to have a gradient to mimic a water's edge. In one place the water should be deep enough for the terrapin to float vertically in the water, while still being able to just touch the bottom.

• **You can use tap water in the tank** but make sure it is warm enough.

Diet

Terrapins are mainly carnivorous, but also herbivorous. They are demanding feeders and can become very particular – especially if the food is not fresh. Young terrapins need feeding daily but older individuals may only need a meal two to three times a week. They must be fed in the water so you may want to feed them in a separate tank to reduce the number of times you have to change the water. This will also encourage the animals to feed more quickly. In the wild they tend to have rapid bouts of feeding during the warmest part of the day, and they feed in the water. They have large stomachs and long gut to handle big meals that are eaten quickly.

Aim for a varied diet. In the wild they eat: fish, frogs, tadpoles, crustacea such as shrimps and water fleas, insects, molluscs and worms. The following can all be used as part of a varied diet for a pet terrapin: earth worms (not blood worms), whitebait, sprats, oxygenating weed, broad-leaf watercress, prawns in their shells, snails, rabbit, chicken, turkey, crab-sticks, cockles, dead mice and pinkies (dead baby mice), small amounts of kidney and liver and morsels of dog or cat food. A piece of cuttlefish should be left

Peter Heathcote, founder of Proteus Reptile Rescue, gives Big Fella her daily health-check

floating on the water and fresh ingredients should be rubbed with a special vitamin and mineral supplement.

Handling
Hold them around the shell just in front of the back legs or, for very aggressive individuals, grip the back of the shell. Hold them upside down to relax them.

Proteus Reptile Rescue
Peter Heathcote and his staff publish and distribute information to anybody who wants it. Good reptile owners are educated and informed.

You can call or write to Proteus Reptile Rescue (see page 127) for a free fact-sheet on terrapins.

The story of Jensen, the sad puppy

I LOATHE PUPPY FARMERS — AS FAR AS I AM CONCERNED THEY HAVE NO PLACE ON THIS PLANET, AND I'M SURE THAT ALL OF YOU WILL SHARE MY FEELINGS TOWARDS THEM. BUT JUST GETTING HOT UNDER THE COLLAR ABOUT PUPPY FARMS DOES NOTHING FOR THE DOGS THAT HAVE TO ENDURE LIFE INSIDE THEM. FOR THE DOGS' SAKE, PUPPY FARMERS MUST BE PUT OUT OF BUSINESS AND I DON'T BELIEVE THAT DOG LOVERS SHOULD RELY ON THE GOVERNMENT OR ANIMAL-RESCUE ORGANISA- TIONS TO DO IT: IT'S UP TO US. PUPPY FARMS STAY OPEN BECAUSE PEOPLE KEEP BUYING THEIR 'PRODUCT'. THE PEOPLE WHO RUN THEM FEED LIKE PARASITES OFF FOOLISH SOULS WHO WANT A DOG BUT CAN'T BE BOTHERED TO DO THEIR HOMEWORK. IF YOU'RE THINKING OF TAKING ON A PUPPY, MAKE ABSOLUTELY SURE THAT YOU'RE NOT ONE OF THESE IMPULSE BUYERS.

A puppy's early experiences in the first few weeks of life have a profound influence on his future health and behaviour. If that puppy is going to become a well-adjusted family pet, it is best for him if he is born to a healthy, unstressed mother and spends his first weeks in the kind of home he will end up living in. In this environment he will naturally get used to all the sounds and smells in a house, and he will learn to play and socialise with people as well as his litter-mates.

If he is born on a puppy farm, it is very likely that he will not have this happy, healthy introduction to life. Puppy farms are dog-breeding establishments, described by the National Canine Defence League (NCDL), dog welfare charity, as a 'mass and indiscriminate system of pedigree dog breeding'. The puppies are bred purely for profit, and the scale of the operations, plus the speed at which the puppies are taken from their mothers, means there is great concern for the dogs' welfare.

Dogs from puppy farms are never cuddled or treated with affection. They are deprived of contact with their mothers from an early age, unable to exercise, play or even see daylight. They lack the experience of a normal domestic environment, which means that when they are sold as pets they are likely to be timid, afraid and confused when confronted by people, but also by everyday objects like washing machines and vacuum cleaners. Separation from their mothers when too young is also a major handicap for puppy-farm-bred dogs later in life.

Pet behaviour counsellor Sarah Whitehead says, 'Puppies learn vast amounts about social interaction and communication from their mother and litter-mates. Those that are taken away too early will never learn about body language and may be aggressive to their own species later. The ideal time to get a puppy is around seven to eight weeks – certainly a puppy should never be taken from its mother before six weeks of age.'

Jensen is a golden retriever who was bought from a puppy farm in Wales for £150 by a family in Newbury, Berkshire. Tania Plaice and her partner Roland Ashley had never bought a dog before and wanted a family pet for their son. They spotted an advertisement in *Thames Valley Free Ads*, and phoned up. The woman who answered the telephone was well spoken, sounded respectable and agreed to deliver the puppy. Tania and Roland had heard the warnings about the importance of investigating the background of a puppy and meeting its mother, but decided to take a chance.

They agreed to meet the breeder on her way to Reading, at a mutually convenient time in a service station. The breeder carried Jensen to their car claiming that he couldn't be put down on the floor because he hadn't been inoculated. 'I knew immediately that something was wrong,' says Tania. 'In the car Jensen was fearful and whimpering, and when we got him home he couldn't place his back leg on the floor.' They immediately called the vet and the next day it appeared that Jensen not only had a fractured leg, but also severe diarrhoea: he went to the toilet up to twenty times a day and was passing blood. Although the breeder claimed that Jensen had been wormed recently, when Tania wormed the dog again, she was appalled to see how many he passed. He was unresponsive and timid and Tania and Roland were afraid that Jensen's behavioural problems might put their child in danger. 'I was terribly torn,' says Tania; 'we really wanted to keep the dog, but the vet's bills were mounting up and it was just one thing after another.'

Tania and Roland spent £500 at their vet's, but Jensen was still having problems, and they did not know how to cope with their troubled little puppy. They felt they had spent all the money they could afford on him. Like many people who buy a puppy on impulse it seems that they had failed to plan for the possibility that their new puppy might become ill or injured! In desperation they took him, now fifteen weeks old, to RSPCA Millbrook. They signed his care over to the RSPCA. 'It was awful: we were so upset, but Jensen was

obviously not right and we just couldn't cope,' says Tania. 'We knew that a dog would cost time and money, but we were stretched to the limit and worried that he [Jensen] might turn on our son.'

Unlike a normal, bouncy retriever puppy, Jensen just sat and remained in a depressed stupor when he arrived at Millbrook. He would not eat in front of anybody and didn't want to play. The next few weeks were crucial if Jensen was to have any chance of developing into a well-adjusted dog who could be rehomed.

Sadly, it is often dogs like Jensen, most in need of a loving family, who are the hardest to home. Potential owners are afraid that they will not be able to cope with the puppy's problems, especially if young children are involved – it's a Catch–22 situation.

With the dedication of the RSPCA team at Millbrook, particularly volunteer Joan Stubblefield, Jensen was taught how to socialise with other dogs and play. 'I remember clearly when he first came in and we weighed him,' says Joan, 'he just froze on the scale, went into a catatonic state. Only when another dog walked past did he begin to move around a bit and behave

Jensen feels at home with his new family in Surrey, which includes four humans and three other dogs

normally. His only experiences of humans had been traumatic; bundled into the back of a car with a broken leg and then taken to a home with a young child. He was terrified.'

Joan started socialising Jensen by bringing her own old mongrel Big Max to meet him. She explains that they were the perfect foil for one another: 'Max is not the kind of dog who is going to get excited or turn on a young puppy; if another dog gets too excited he'll give a small growl, but he's friendly and patient. Gradually, Jensen began to come out of himself a bit.' Slowly, Joan helped Jensen build up confidence: 'We started off in the hall playing with toys and getting him to retrieve, then as his confidence grew, took him into the compound to play with other dogs.'

Jensen also attended puppy classes, but Sarah Whitehead, who ran the class, feared he would never completely recover. 'Jensen's behaviour was typical of a puppy who had been kept in a deprived environment throughout the most critical stages of his development. He showed distressing symptoms of withdrawal from human contact, consistent with a lack of frequent and pleasant exposure and handling by people when it mattered most.' Miraculously, however, he slowly began to respond to other dogs and become more alert. Gradually he improved and finally started to come out of his shell. Now he needed a good family who were prepared to carry on the good work started at Millbrook.

Meanwhile, Jensen's original owners, Tania and Roland, had been telephoning the breeder who supplied Jensen. Although she'd originally agreed to pay the veterinary costs Tania and Roland had incurred, she cut off all contact and refused to take their calls when the bill was sent. Not surprisingly, she never paid up. Tania and Roland are now taking the breeder to court. When Tania contacted *Thames Valley Free Ads* to inform the paper of the situation, it appeared that she was not the first to have lodged a complaint about this particular breeder, although she is certainly the first to have taken such direct action.

The Trading Standards Office has been contacted in an attempt to ban the breeder from advertising, and with the RSPCA it is attempting to get an injunction to prevent her trading. The chief inspector of the South Wales RSPCA believes there may be a case against the breeder for mistreatment. RSPCA inspectors have made several visits to her premises, but each time the breeder herds her dogs into the house and tells the RSPCA if they want to enter her home they will need to contact her solicitor. The solicitor of course denies access and the inspectors have to keep turning up on the off-chance.

The staff at Millbrook were concerned that no one had shown any interest in Jensen, but then Jennifer McGuiness turned up. A local woman who has rescued other dogs from the RSPCA, she first heard about Jensen through her son's girlfriend, who was doing work experience at Millbrook as part of her veterinary training. The girlfriend knew immediately that Jennifer would fall in love with Jensen. She was right. As Jennifer says, 'He was lovely. I just knew we could give him a good home and that he'd benefit from living with the other dogs.' But first, because the RSPCA hadn't checked their home for two years, they had to make a home visit to make sure that the McGuinesses could offer Jensen the kind of lifestyle he needed.

Jensen and the other dogs belonging to the McGuinesses are exercised three times a day, and Jensen loves running free off the lead

As expected, the home visit was a success. The RSPCA could see that Neil and Jennifer McGuiness had a spacious, comfortable, loving environment to offer Jensen. They have four sons, two of whom still live at home, and three other dogs: Henry an eight-year-old golden retriever, and two year-old cross dalmatians, Basil and Barney, who were both rescued from the RSPCA. The cross dalmatians are very close to one another and Jensen has struck up a special bond with Henry. 'I think he thinks that Henry is his dad – they're constantly playing together, rolling around on the floor.'

The McGuinesses are totally committed to their dogs and exercise them three times a day. Each dog has a basket in the kitchen where they sleep all night, but otherwise they all have the run of the house – as well as the garden. The dogs chase around together and have tremendous fun. When

*All dogs love to explore new environments on their walks, and Jensen is no exception.
The McGuinesses' other dogs make walks even more fun*

he first arrived at his new home Jensen was still a little timid: 'His tail was down all the time, even at feeding,' said Jennifer, 'but now he's constantly wagging his tail in happiness. He was a little bit nervous at first, but now he's just like any other puppy I've ever had.'

With love and commitment, some puppy-farmed dogs can be rehabilitated and Jensen was one of the lucky ones. Thousands like him, however, continue to suffer and the only way to help these dogs is to ensure that this cruel trade is stopped.

Puppy farming in the UK

According to the NCDL, the practice of puppy farming has reached epidemic proportions in the UK. In the last ten years it has grown from a small cottage industry into big business. Although it is impossible to put a figure on the proportion of pure-bred dogs that come from these establishments, the NCDL estimates that there are 1,000 puppy farms in West Wales alone, with reports of new farms springing up in southern Ireland and Scotland. Together they are breeding up to 70,000 puppies a year for profit – and this could be just the tip of the iceberg.

The large-scale breeding of dogs on puppy farms and their subsequent sale causes a number of welfare concerns. Puppies are often taken from their mothers too early; adult dogs are kept in cramped or unsuitable conditions; bitches are bred from too often, jeopardising their health; dogs are often given insufficient exercise or human contact and the long-distance transportation of puppies from the farms can cause severe distress.

According to NCDL spokesman Nick Southall: 'Any pure-bred dog you see for sale in a pet shop, or any dealer you come across that offers more than two breeds for sale is a sure indication that the dogs have come from a puppy farm. Reputable breeders never have more than two breeds, and will show the puppy with its mother and litter-mates.'

Under the Breeding of Dogs Acts 1973 and 1991, breeding establishments with two or more breeding bitches should obtain a licence from the local authority, which must be satisfied that certain conditions are fulfilled before granting a licence, assessing such factors as building, size, cleanliness, exercise arrangements, food, drink and bedding materials.

According to the NCDL, up to 57 per cent of puppy farms in some areas are not licensed, and even those that are can legitimately produce puppies in conditions that are totally inappropriate for dogs destined to become family pets. It maintains that local authority inspections are likely to be carried out by Environmental Health Officers, qualified only to judge the condition of the premises, not the condition of the dogs. As the law stands, breeders can only be prosecuted on the grounds of environmental health, or once there is evidence that suffering has taken place. A Parliamentary Bill tabled by Liberal Democrat MP Diana Maddock in January 1997 called for the introduction of legislation to prosecute unlicensed dog breeders, but unfortunately it made no progress and was dropped.

A typical puppy farm has about thirty breeding bitches on the premises, with the largest farms having up to 150. The most commonly farmed breeds are German shepherds, rottweilers, labradors, golden retrievers, spaniels and varieties of terrier. They are often kept in cramped and filthy conditions in damp cattle sheds or pigsties, deprived of daylight, affection and exercise. The bitches are forced to have litter after litter (typically two a year) for their entire breeding lives, usually about eight years, with little or no human contact. The NCDL has found that once the bitches are bred to exhaustion and no longer hold any value for the farmers, they are disposed of either by being put down, or dumped at animal rescue centres.

Not surprisingly, this kind of lifestyle takes its toll on body and mind, and the puppies of these exhausted bitches cannot develop normally. Sarah Whitehead makes a comparison: 'Imagine taking a child, and placing him or her in a cupboard for five years. During this time you feed the child and give him water, but that is all. If, after five years we took the child out of the cupboard, would we really expect that child to be a normal social being? This may appear to be an extreme example, but put in the context of what happens to many pet dogs it is perhaps a good analogy.'

Breeders make on average £3000 from a litter of pure-bred puppies and try to increase profit margins by cutting costs. The dogs receive little or no veterinary attention and often are not even given the necessary vaccinations. Additional health problems may occur because puppy farmers have little knowledge about dog health and behaviour and are not selective about which dogs they breed. A spokesman for the British Veterinary Assocation (BVA), Paul DeVile says: 'Conditions on unlicensed puppy farms are either unsuitable or appalling. The bitches are bred from too often with no thought of the genetic dangers of in-breeding. The premises are, in the main, old farm buildings, encouraging the spread of disease, and the puppies suffer additional stress when taken from the mother and transported long distances to be sold via a dealer or retail outlet. If dogs were bred properly, under licence, in proper conditions there would be little to complain about. As things stand now, it's a trade that must be stamped out.'

Puppy farming at its worst –
the case of Helen Hein

An appalling case of puppy farming cruelty was exposed by Inspector Alison MacVicar. It involved a former Ministry of Agriculture vet, sixty-nine-year-old Helen Hein, who kept 140 German shepherd dogs cooped up in a filthy house and outbuilding caked with as much as three inches of dog muck on the floors. The dogs had grouped into packs which Dr Hein had little control over. Some of the dogs had injuries from dog fights that went untreated; others were possibly deformed from in-breeding. Some of them were locked up in tiny cages. When they died, she would dump the bodies in black plastic bags and leave them out for the dustmen.

For at least fifteen years, clients had paid up to £400 for a puppy from the unlicensed Hein after answering her advertisements in the local free ads. Ads placed by puppy farmers or dealers can be seen in almost any local paper or free sheet, although in their efforts to warn the public of unscrupulous dog traders, editors are now placing riders above the ads that warn potential buyers to insist on seeing puppies with their mothers before purchase.

Many of Hein's buyers reported pets so traumatised by their first few weeks of life that they had long-term behavioural dificulties. Customers were not allowed to enter the premises, and puppies would be handed over at the front gate. Alison MacVicar tried several times to inspect Hein's squalid premises

near Guildford after tip-offs from suspicious buyers, but was consistently denied access. Finally, with the help of a warrant from Guildford Borough Council, Alison gained entry, and was shocked by what she found. 'I just couldn't believe it – it was completely unreal. I have never been so appalled, upset and angry at any sight of animal suffering before or since.'

Alison's boss, Superintendent Alan Goddard, claims it was the worst cruelty case he had seen in twenty years. Hein did not use bowls for the dog food, but merely threw it on the filthy, mess-covered floor for the dogs to fight over. The amount of water given to the dogs was severely restricted, as Hein believed that giving dogs constant access to water had a bad effect on their stomachs – a quirky and unorthodox view not supported by science. Alison recalls seeing one of the dogs licking the inside of a window on a rainy day. 'It was so sad, the poor thing was torturing itself.'

Helen Hein was successfully prosecuted and banned from having custody of dogs for seven years, but Alison believes that such punishments do not really act as a deterrent. She claims that the worst offenders simply 'move premises and set up somewhere else and carry on. It's completely sickening.' Hein was particularly upset to be struck off by the Royal College of Veterinary Surgeons, and in a statement spoke of her disappointment: 'Although not in

Inspector Alison MacVicar found Helen Hein's dogs living in squalor near Guildford. The Alsatians lived almost wild, roaming the premises in packs

practice, I value my membership of the RCVS, together with my close association with dogs and their owners. I have never considered that I have been cruel to my dogs. I have done everything possible for their care and there was nothing else I could have done.'

Giving evidence at the trial, William Turner, veterinary surgeon and owner of one of the largest boarding kennels in south-west England, said: 'She loves her dogs and her dogs love her. But she acquired more dogs than she could cope with.' Even Alison MacVicar admitted that she loved the dogs – 'they were the family she never had'.

What you can do to stop puppy farming

There is an All-Party Parliamentary Group for Animal Welfare backed up by the Kennel Club, the RSPCA, the NCDL and the BVA, which are attempting to curb puppy farming through legislation, but it is an uphill battle that needs your help if it is to succeed.

These farms rely on you, the buyer, for their survival. From reading this chapter you should be armed with enough knowledge to identify a puppy farm.

Do not be reassured by puppy farmers that can prove the dog is registered with the Kennel Club – as Paul DeVile of the BVA says, 'It should always be remembered that a Kennel Club registration document is simply a statement that the parents were themselves Kennel Club registered. It has no bearing on the conditions in which a puppy has been reared.'

If dog lovers stop buying puppies from puppy farms and stand up and refuse to support this cruel trade, it will cease. Below are some suggestions to help put an end to this immoral business:

• **Contact the RSPCA** and report anyone you suspect of being an unlicensed or inhumane breeder.
• **Write to your MP** – For every letter an MP receives, they assume that there are at least another 100 people in their constituencies who feel the same way. If an MP receives just a dozen letters, this can be enough to get questions asked in the House of Commons. You can find out who your local MP is by telephoning your local council and then writing to him or her at the House of Commons, London SW1A 0AA.
• **Write to the editor** of your local paper and ask them to refuse advertisements from puppy farms or their dealers. Reputable breeders usually specialise in one breed only or two similar breeds – adverts that offer

multiple breeds of dog are likely to be for puppy farms. If you suspect that somebody advertising is a puppy farm breeder, report them to the Trading Standards Office.

• **Persuade your local paper** to print free warning columns in the pets section of the paper, for example 'If you are considering buying a pedigree puppy, always make sure that you see it with its mother, and check the mother's pedigree registration that she is actually the dog she is supposed to be.'

• **Visit your local pet shop** and ask if they sell puppies and if so where they buy their puppies from; contact the RSPCA or the NCDL and let them know.

• **Local councils** can prosecute unlicensed or badly run puppy farms if they have enough evidence, so if you know about puppy farms in your area, please let the council know, or contact your local RSPCA centre.

If you would like to be actively involved in campaigning on this issue, contact the NCDL (address on page 127), or the RSPCA.

Finding a puppy

Once you have decided what type of dog you want, a decision that you should be prepared to put a great deal of time and effort into, you can start looking for possible places where you might be able to obtain a suitable puppy of that sort. If you have decided that you would like a young pure-bred puppy from a litter, your aim for now should be to find the breeding bitch who you would like to be the mother of your new puppy. In appearance, and more importantly temperament, she should be exactly the sort of dog you would like to own yourself. If possible, you should also try to meet the male dog who has been chosen to mate with her. He too, should be the kind of dog that you would want your puppy to be like as an adult.

Pure-bred litters are often booked up in advance by keen would-be owners, so be prepared to join a waiting list. On the other hand, if you want a cross-bred or mongrel puppy of the same age, it is less likely that you will have to wait long for your puppy. As most matings between different breeds or cross-breeds of dog are unplanned, you are unlikely to have the opportunity to choose the mother of your puppy before she is pregnant. You are far more likely to end up looking at the litter of puppies and the bitch at the same time. But try not to get too distracted by the puppies. Unless they are already several weeks old, it is their mother who you need to concentrate on at this stage.

Avoid taking young children on these first visits. They may be very disappointed if you decide that either the bitch or her puppies are unsuitable in any way. A proper search will take time and effort.

If you want a pure-bred puppy

• **Contact the national club** that represents the breed that you are interested in. They should be able to put you in touch with breeders in your area and beyond. Look in dog magazines or ask at your local veterinary centre for a contact telephone number. The staff at your veterinary centre may already know of some of the more local breeders.

• **Visit local, regional and even national dog shows** – You will make lots of useful contacts and will be able to chat to breeders and meet their dogs.

• **If you have a friend who owns a dog** of the breed that you are interested in and you think her dog is just great, find out where she got him from. If possible, take a look at his pedigree and make a note of his father's name. If you ever come across his name again, you will have the benefit of having personally met one of his offspring.

• **Look in the classified sections of local papers** – Many people who own pregnant bitches but do not consider themselves professional dog breeders will advertise litters before they are born. (But beware of advertisements put in by puppy farmers – see pages 85 and 88.)

• **Make a shortlist of possible breeders** with suitable bitches and then make arrangements to visit them all. Try to find out which male dogs the breeders have chosen to mate with the bitches that you are interested in. If you can, visit them.

• **When you go to see a bitch on your shortlist** don't just concentrate on the bitch herself. Take a long, hard look at her owner and the way she interacts with her dogs. You should get a good impression of how she will treat your puppy in his early weeks. Ask for the names of other people who have bought puppies from her so that you can find out later if they had any problems that were possibly related to the way in which they were reared. Expect to be cross-examined by the breeder. A good breeder will want to be sure every available puppy goes to a caring and suitable home. You should be very suspicious if you are not questioned by the breeder.

• **Some breeds of dog suffer from serious conditions** such as hip abnormalities, that are known to be passed on from generation to generation. For some of these, there are tests that can be done on breeding animals in order to identify those dogs and bitches that are most likely to pass on the problem to their puppies. Before visiting any bitch of the breed that you are interested in, ask your vet if there are any special questions that you should ask her owner about both the bitch and the dog.

• **Although it may seem more convenient** to obtain your puppy from a friend than to carry out a proper search, don't agree to do so simply because it is an easy option. Compromise on looks, but never on temperament.

• **Avoid restricting your search** for breeding bitches just to your local area. It may well be that there are only a few breeding bitches of the breed that you are interested in living nearby. Be prepared to travel further afield to find the perfect parents for your puppy.

• **Animal rescue organisations** have litters of pure-bred puppies available for rehoming from time to time. If you would rather rescue a puppy then keep in touch with the good rescue centres in your area and the national rescue organisations for the breed you are interested in. Be cautious about young puppies that are not with their mother. It may be very difficult for you to judge their temperament.

If you want a cross-bred, or mongrel puppy

• **Look in the classified sections of your local papers** for advertisements for litters that are due, or for puppies that are already available. The puppies should not be more than eight weeks old and bear in mind what you now know about puppy farms and the way they advertise.

• **Contact dog rescue organisations** in your area and your local vet centres. They may be looking after, or may know of, a pregnant bitch or one that has had her puppies. Rescue centres may also have orphaned puppies that need homes, but if you are a first-time dog owner, you should really avoid puppies who are not with their mother. These puppies are often better off in the care of more experienced dog owners.

• **If possible, visit several pregnant bitches** to meet them and their owners. Your choice may be limited in your area, so if none of the bitches on your initial shortlist meets your expectations, be patient and keep looking or begin to search further afield.

• **Be prepared** – If you meet a bitch with a litter of puppies who are already several weeks old and you like her, her puppies and her owner, you may have to decide on a particular puppy sooner than you had planned. But don't miss out any of the important preparation stages detailed in the next few pages.

If you want an older puppy

You will need to carry out the same sort of research as if you were searching to obtain either a pure-bred or cross-bred six- to eight-week-old puppy (see above).

Choosing your new companion

If possible, try to visit the litter of puppies from which you want to choose your puppy a number of times before you make your final decision. You will then get a much better impression of the characters of the individual puppies. Remember that there is no single 'best' puppy in a litter: each one will have its own good points and bad points.

Most dog behaviour experts agree that the best age for a puppy to be adopted and moved to his new home is when he is six to eight weeks old. At that age, he is in the middle of an important period of his mental development, called the socialisation period. Adoption before six weeks old may affect his future relationships with other dogs. Remaining with his litter too long and not moving to his new home until after he is eight weeks old, may in the long-term affect the way he relates to people. For that very reason, those who train guide dogs for the blind usually home all their puppies with volunteer families at the age of six weeks in order to improve the chances of the puppies becoming mentally well-adjusted successful guide dogs. The American Guide Dogs for the Blind found that of puppies kept in their kennels until twelve weeks old only around one in three were suitable to go on to become fully-fledged guide dogs.

Step one – Arrange to make your final visit to see the litter when they are between six and eight weeks old. If you are planning to take your puppy home on the same day as you choose him, try to make the visit on a day when you are going to be around at home for at least the next couple of days to look after him. Also, make your visit as early in the day as possible so that your puppy has the whole day to get used to you and your home before you put him to bed. Make sure that when you go, there will be no other prospective owners around to distract you, the breeder, the puppies or their mother.

If possible, all those who are going to live with your puppy and help look after him should go along with you. But any children must be old enough to understand the importance of the decision that you are about to make. Make sure that they understand what to do when you all get there and make it clear that you will make the final decision. Warn the breeder that you will want to observe the puppies from a distance before you take a closer look at them.

Step two – If you will be taking your new puppy home on the same day, make sure that you are completely prepared for him at home, that you have the right equipment to take him home in the car and that if at all possible you have arranged an appointment for him to be checked over by your vet on the way home.

Step three – When you arrive, spend fifteen to twenty minutes just watching the litter playing together and interacting with the breeder and their mother. Some of the puppies may already be chosen, so make sure that the breeder points out to you which ones are still available. Try to form an opinion as to the temperament of each of the puppies that are available for you to choose from. Some puppies are obviously quieter than others.

Some are definitely shy, while others are full of their own self-confidence. Ask the breeder what she thinks of each of the puppies. She sees the puppies every day and she has witnessed them growing up. Explain what kind of puppy you want and a responsible breeder should help you select a puppy that will be well-suited to you.

If you are a first-time dog owner, it may be best to avoid the most outgoing puppy, as he may prove to be a bit of a handful. A shy, timid puppy may not be a good idea if you will expect him to live in a busy, bustling household. For most families, a puppy that is not too cocky but not too shy and retiring is a good choice. Remember that a puppy's behaviour is likely to be influenced by his litter mates. An apparently shy puppy that finds one or more of his brothers and sisters a little overpowering may come right out of his shell when away from the rest of his litter. If there are only one or two puppies to choose from of the right sex, and you are not happy about the temperament of either of them, say so. You are under no obligation to take one of them and you may be much better off arranging to have the pick of the next or another litter.

Step four – Ask the breeder if you can have a closer look at the puppies of the right sex that are still available. You should have spent some time getting to know the puppies' mother on previous visits, so she and the rest of the litter can be put away somewhere where they won't distract you. Spend some time interacting with all the puppies that you have shortlisted. But, rather than actively playing with them, just sit on the ground to start with and see how they interact with you. Again confirm in your own mind which one is the boldest. Is the puppy that you thought to be a little timid hanging back? Once they have got used to you, play with them a little. A strong-minded puppy may want to take control of games and will play with absolute confidence. Such a puppy may be best suited to a more experienced owner.

Once you have spent some time with them all together, take a closer look at them individually. Carry out a simple health check on each puppy. Use your common sense. Your aim should be just to make sure that there is nothing obviously wrong with any of the puppies. If in doubt about anything, ask the breeder. And don't forget that your vet should thoroughly check the puppy that you finally choose for any potentially serious problems that you may miss.

Step five – It's decision time. Making the final choice is never easy. You will probably want to take them all home. If there are only two to choose from and you are finding it difficult to make up your mind, you may be tempted to take them both because of guilt feelings about leaving one puppy on his own. Don't. Stick by your original decision about numbers and sex. The breeder will make sure that all the puppies go to good homes. Have a family conference if necessary, but make sure that in the event of a split decision, you have all agreed that it is you who will have the casting vote.

Step six – Once you have made your decision, inform the breeder, but explain that your decision is subject to the approval of your vet. A good breeder should have no problem with that. Make sure that when you leave with your puppy, you have all of the following:

• **A receipt** for the amount of money that you have paid.

• **Your puppy's pedigree registration papers** (if any).

• **Insurance documents** (if any). Some breeders take out a short-term health insurance on all their puppies which is transferable to new owners.

• **Vaccination record** (if any). Some puppies may have started their vaccination course early.

• **Worming record** including the timing of any worming procedures carried out and the product or products used.

• **Medical record** including details of any other treatments carried out by the breeder or her vet.

• **Feeding notes** to include details of current foods being offered and timings and size of meals. Ask if you can buy or take with you some of the puppy's current food items so that you can slowly change over to the new food that you have chosen.

• **A piece of your puppy's bedding** so that he will have something that smells familiar in his new home.

Choosing a young puppy from a rescue centre

If you are an inexperienced dog owner and you are interested in a young puppy at a rescue centre, but his mother is not around for you to see, I recommend that you seek the advice of an animal behaviour expert before deciding to take him on.

Choosing an older puppy

It is unlikely that you will be able to see an older puppy with his mother. Spend time with any older puppy that you are interested in. Play with him and take him for a walk. If you think that a particular puppy is wonderful and will suit you well, but you are inexperienced with dogs and would like a second opinion, why not ask a veterinary nurse or animal behaviour expert to come along and have a look at the puppy with you. Many of the best animal rescue centres now employ animal behaviour experts to help match would-be owners to dogs needing new homes.

Peggy and Bob: innocent victims of cruelty

I'LL NEVER FORGET THE FIRST TIME I HAD TO AMPUTATE A CAT'S FRONT LEG. ALTHOUGH I KNEW THAT DOING SO WOULD SAVE THE CAT'S LIFE, I WAS SO WORRIED THAT HE WOULDN'T COPE AFTER THE OPERATION. I WAS NOT LONG QUALIFIED AND ALL MY MORE EXPERIENCED COLLEAGUES REASSURED ME THAT HE WOULD BE FINE. AND, OF COURSE, THEY WERE RIGHT. SO WHEN I FIRST MET PEGGY, JUST HOURS AFTER HER FRONT LEG HAD BEEN AMPUTATED, I FELT SURE THAT SHE WOULD QUICKLY BOUNCE BACK. HOW WRONG I WAS. SHE NOT ONLY BOUNCED, BUT LEAPT, JUMPED, RAN AND RACED BACK TO FULL FITNESS IN RECORD TIME. HER RECOVERY WAS INCREDIBLE. SADLY, BOB'S AMPUTATION WAS DONE BY AMATEURS AND HIS WAS A VERY DIFFERENT STORY.

Peggy: a cat with only eight lives left

RSPCA inspectors are all too often called upon to help both wild animals and pets that have suffered severe injuries through being caught in indiscriminate snares or improperly used spring traps set by hunters to catch rabbits and foxes, animals that they see as pests. If Peggy had not been found when she was, she would have died a slow and agonising death.

In autumn 1996 three people out walking in Surrey found a young tabby-and-white kitten with one of her front legs caught in a spring trap. Very distressed, the walkers contacted the RSPCA. When Inspector Jason Giddings arrived, he released her from the trap, but could feel that her injured leg was cold and lifeless. He suspected nerve damage, and rushed her to veterinary surgeon Kate Murphy in nearby Guildford. Kate did her best to save the kitten's leg, but knew that the outlook was bleak: 'The kitten herself was quite bright, but the leg was a mess, covered with maggots. By the Monday it had become gangrenous and had to be amputated.'

Kate performed the operation. All went well and the kitten was soon on the road to recovery. Kate was amazed by the way the kitten coped: 'She sat up straight after surgery. I put in a drain to help get rid of the excess fluid and treated her with antibiotics and painkillers for three or four days before she was moved to Millbrook.'

When the kitten arrived at RSPCA Millbrook, deputy manager Sue Walters was astounded by the little cat's resilience: 'She was an extremely good-natured cat, purring away and eager for human contact. We wanted her to acclimatise gradually, so at first we kept her in a small cage so she couldn't move around too much and strain herself. After a little while we moved her into the cattery where she adapted very well.'

Sue named the little cat Peggy, and RSPCA staff decided that it would be best for Peggy to recover at home rather than being kept in the cattery. To find where Peggy lived, though, meant finding her owner first. Knocking on doors in the area near where the walkers discovered Peggy produced no results. Nobody seemed to know anything about the cat. She was scanned for an identifying microchip (see page 121 for more on microchips) but the scanner found nothing, and she was not wearing any other form of identification. In desperation, the RSPCA called in a local paper to do a front-page spread with photographs in an effort to find her owner. Nobody came forward.

The RSPCA decided to prosecute the landowner responsible for setting the trap that caught Peggy. The pathologist in Peggy's case, George Tribe, gave evidence in court demonstrating that Peggy had suffered acutely – he estimated that she had spent three days in the trap before her discovery and that the pain that led up to the gangrenous state of her limb and eventual amputation was enormous. The landowner pleaded guilty in April 1997 and sustained fines and costs.

Peggy was finally adopted by Catherine Moore, a Millbrook voluntary worker who lives nearby. Catherine works at the centre on Sundays, cleaning out cages and walking the dogs. Peggy has since been renamed Lillian after Catherine's grandmother, who had recently broken her hip – Catherine saw a parallel in their situations. Lillian now shares her new home with two other cats, thirteen-year-old Jessie and four-year-old Mo. Mo was also rescued by the RSPCA. Catherine had absolutely no reservations about taking on a disabled cat: 'She was such a nice, friendly cat with a wonderful character.'

In her new home Lillian is feeling a million dollars and is full of mischief. So far she has scratched the furniture, climbed up the shirts in the wardrobe and

fallen into the swing bin, from which she was quickly removed! She is extremely playful and has mixed well with the other cats, although Jessie is a bit old for playing with such an energetic kitten. Catherine reckons that Lillian is already the boss in her home, and Lillian has a particular fondness for climbing onto the back of people's necks and snuggling in. Catherine is well aware that disabled cats like Lillian need special care, and keeps her in while she's at work, but has decided not to confine her indoors all the time. 'She seems as capable as a four-legged cat: I try not to let her out the front because of traffic, but we let her out the back and she doesn't seem to notice that she has a leg missing; she scales the fence and runs around – she's unstoppable.'

Catherine Moore, a voluntary worker at RSPCA Millbrook, adopted Peggy and renamed her Lillian after her grandmother

Snares, spring traps and their victims

Snares are among the most cruel and indiscriminate killers of wild and domestic animals, but they are not illegal. A snare is simply a wire noose, one end of which is attached to a stake or heavy object that acts as an anchor.

They are usually set to catch foxes or rabbits, but their victims are quite often other animals, including badgers, dogs and even unsuspecting cats. The RSPCA estimates that sometimes only a third of all animals caught in snares are actually 'target species'. A spring trap is, as its name implies, triggered by the movement of an animal across it. The leg-hold or 'gin trap' has been banned in Britain since 1958, but other forms of spring trap are legal, if used properly, against certain species. Being used properly means that they must be set within natural or artificial tunnels to avoid animals such as Peggy becoming trapped by the leg.

By law, landowners who set traps and snares are obliged to check them at least once a day. The RSPCA believes that this is often disregarded, which means that the animal may spend days trying to escape – an almost impossible task. A snared animal is usually caught by the neck or leg, and once caught, it panics and struggles to get away. The more it struggles, the tighter the noose becomes. The tighter the noose, the more the animal suffers. Victims of snares may die quickly through strangulation, but many animals caught in both snares and traps suffer a lingering demise. Those that are rescued from illegal gin traps or illegally set spring traps almost always lose a limb. If an animal is caught for several days, it will die as a result of its injuries, of thirst or hunger, or be killed by another animal. Sometimes an animal succeeds in pulling the snare away from the anchor and escapes with the wire still firmly attached to it, only to die later from its injuries. The RSPCA receives many reports of cats and protected animals such as badgers that have been caught in snares. Similar reports on foxes show horrific injuries caused by snares used in the name of pest control.

Because snares cause so much suffering, it may be hard to understand why they aren't made illegal. But landowners argue that a well-set-up and regularly checked snare or trap is the best way of catching the animals they regard as pests. The Wildlife and Countryside Act of 1981 states that users of snares and traps must take 'all reasonable precautions' to prevent injury to protected animals, but these 'reasonable precautions' can never guarantee that non-target species will avoid traps. Like me, the RSPCA is opposed to the manufacture and use of all snares and any trap that causes suffering, and believes that there are humane alternatives of pest control. Cage traps, for example, which leave the animal alive and uninjured, have proved to be an effective and humane method of catching rabbits.

Caring for a three-legged cat

A cat's front legs have built in shock-absorbers! They are not connected to the rest of the cat's skeleton by bone, but simply by

muscles. When a cat jumps down and lands on her front legs these muscles help to reduce the stresses and strains that she has to cope with when she makes contact with the ground. Cats like Lillian, with only one front leg, are more vulnerable to athletic injuries and are less able to make an escape when they feel threatened – for instance by another cat, dog or even car. As a result, it is very important for owners of three-legged cats to consider very carefully the kind of exercise that their cats should be allowed to take. Every case has to be dealt with on its own merits, but some cats with three legs may be best kept confined.

If you have a disabled cat then you may have no choice but to keep her indoors all the time, or restrict her outdoor forays to a large, secure cage. But you won't be on your own. These days, many owners of able-bodied cats choose to restrict their cats' movements for a whole variety of reasons, including fears about busy roads and the possibility of their cats getting involved in fights with others.

Those who do choose to have so-called 'house-cats' must take on the added responsibility of entertaining their pets' minds as well as giving them plenty of opportunity to exercise. For most cats the great outdoors provides all the natural stimulation they need. Indoors, life tends to be rather predictable and more than a little boring. But it doesn't have to be that way, and in my experience happy house-cats have imaginative owners!

You should make the decision about whether or not you are going to keep your cat permanently indoors before you bring her home. Of course, you can change your mind, but it may be more difficult for your cat to adjust to life indoors, especially if she is a young kitten, if you allow her outside at first and then subsequently decide to keep her as an indoor pet. A young kitten who has not experienced life outdoors is likely to adjust better to having her movements restricted than an older kitten who already knows about life on the other side of the cat flap. It is a decision that you should not make lightly.

The following are some of the things that you should consider:
• **The kind of cat you have chosen** and her suitability to an outdoor lifestyle. For obvious reasons, certain longer-haired cats such as Persians have coats that look beautiful when well cared for, but that are not very well adapted to scrambling and stalking through dense undergrowth.
• **The resident pet, feral and farm cat population** in your neighbourhood. Ask at your vet centre for their view of the frequency of local cat fights.
• **Your local environment** for instance, the proximity of roads and other transport routes that may constitute major hazards to your cat.

Lillian is a trusting and inquisitive cat who likes to explore her environment. She's even climbed up the clothes in the wardrobe!

• **The need that all cats share** for the kind of physical and mental stimulation that an outdoor lifestyle offers.

• **The responsibility that you have as a cat owner** to offer your cat as many lifestyle choices as you can.

Remember that you do have the option of giving your kitten restricted access outdoors in a large and secure garden enclosure. You can make one yourself out of wood and netting, or you can buy one. Inside there should be lots to interest your cat – scratching posts, sleeping platforms, enclosed areas, toys – and, of course, a litter tray.

Life indoors

Cats kept indoors permanently must be able to occupy themselves doing the same kinds of things for the same amount of time as they would if they had free access outside. It is impossible to work out what is best for your cat without having an understanding of some of her natural physical and behavioural needs.

Sleep

Cats are completely natural sleepers ! At least eight, and up to twelve hours a day is the general rule. Older cats may snooze for as many as sixteen hours a day. This does not mean that cats are lazy. They are simply obeying nature's golden rule that a well-fed carnivore should keep itself out of sight, both to keep hidden from rivals of its own species and to avoid scaring away potential prey. As most pet cats are offered a plentiful and readily accessible supply of tasty food on a regular and frequent schedule, many cats may be close to a soporific state almost permanently!

Unlike people, cats do not do all their sleeping in a single period during the night. Instead, they really do 'cat-nap', splitting their sleep into several bouts spread out over the whole twenty-four hours. They are usually most active at dawn and dusk, and are most likely to sleep in the middle of the night and the middle of the day. But this routine is weather-dependent, and in the winter cats may sleep mainly at night and restrict their outdoor activity to daylight hours.

In one respect their sleep is very like ours. It consists of alternating periods of light sleep, from which a cat sleeps peacefully but is easily woken, and deeper sleep, when she is much less easy to wake. The deep sleep is also known as 'paradoxical' sleep, because although the cat is completely limp for most of the time, occasionally her tail, whiskers or paws may twitch, or her eyes flicker. This is just what people do when they are dreaming, so we can speculate that cats also dream when they are sleeping deeply.

So, your cat needs:
• **A choice of sleeping locations** in out-of-the-way places where she will not be disturbed. Some should be in warmer spots than others and some off the ground to provide her with a greater feeling of security.
• **A choice of bedding materials** (ideally).
• **The opportunity to reach her sleeping places** twenty-four hours a day so that she can cat-nap when she wants to.

Food

Feral cats hunt and feed several times a day because their natural food is concentrated in small packages and their digestive system is relatively short. An active cat weighing 3.5kg needs about 300 kilocalories a day. As an average mouse provides about 30 kilocalories, it would be fair to assume that cats on a diet of mice would need ten meals every twenty-four hours. Most pet cats fed on commercially pre-prepared cat food also seem to prefer to eat many small meals during the day – between four and twelve depending on the individual cat and the precise formulation of the food they eat. This is particularly true for the growing kitten, which will find it difficult to eat enough if it is only fed once or twice a day. The majority of cats, and almost all kittens, are excellent calorie-counters and will not over-eat even if food is constantly available. Pet cats appear to have a need to hunt even if they are not hungry. Given the opportunity, many cats will set off on a hunting expedition immediately after eating at home. In fact, well-fed house cats allowed free access outdoors may well spend a quarter of each day on hunting expeditions.

So, your cat needs:
- **Access to one or more foods** that together provide for all her nutritional needs.
- **The opportunity to eat several small meals** per day if she wants to.
- **The opportunity to use her predatory hunting instincts** and skills on real or imaginary prey (see 'toys' below).

Play
During the first year of their lives, kittens are naturally very playful. At five months old a kitten may spend up to three hours each day involved in games of one sort or another. Kittens indulge in three different types of play. 'Locomotor' play consists of running, rolling, jumping and climbing. Given a climbing frame, a young kitten will spend considerably more time clambering on it than an adult cat would. Some kittens and adult cats seem keener on this kind of play than others. 'Object' play involves interaction with inanimate objects. No surprise there! When confronted with novel objects, kittens begin by investigating them with their eyes, noses, tongues and paws and then go on to poke, bat, grasp or toss them in the air – if they can.

Recent research seems to indicate that to all intents and purposes, well-orchestrated object play stimulates cats in a very similar way to natural hunting activities and may reduce a cat's in-built predatory desires. Cats seem to spend most time involved in object play when they are around sixteen weeks old. After that, the amount of this kind of play will depend on the kitten's character and personality.

The third type of play – 'social' play – consists of interaction between kittens. To an outside observer such games may actually look like fights. Fortunately, most play bouts of this kind end amicably! Kittens are most actively involved in social play when they are between nine and fourteen weeks old. Although adult cats tend not to play as much as kittens, most can be encouraged to do so. The benefits of play are enormous – exercise, mental agility and fun to name but three.

So, your cat needs:

- **Suitable toys** to satisfy her need for object play and to help reduce her instinctive desire to hunt.
- **You (or another appropriate animal)** as a partner for social play for the first few weeks.
- **A suitable 'adventure playground'** where she can indulge in locomotor play. Some form of climbing frame is sure to be a real winner.

Toys and other play paraphernalia

You can buy or make for your cat a whole range of play objects or toys. Your cat's toys do not need to be high-tech. Perhaps the best and most successful cat toy of all time is a screwed up piece of paper. It goes without saying that any toy that you buy or make should be strong and safe, as your cat may become quite ferocious while playing, and will certainly try to dismember any toy using her paws and mouth. Any toy that you buy should be labelled with full instructions for use. In general you will get what you pay for! Avoid toys that are sold loose and test the strength of all toys yourself before offering them to your cat.

Don't think that all you have to do to satisfy your cat's play needs is to offer her three or four well-made sophisticated toys and then let him get on with it. Cats, especially adults, become very bored, very quickly with toys. Despite recent scientific studies, experts still do not understand why kittens and cats seem to be endlessly fascinated with real mice, but quickly tire of toy mice. But they are in no doubt that if a kitten is to get the most from playing with toys, she will need the help of her owner – you. You will soon learn the games that your kitten enjoys playing as well as those that quickly bore her.

The following are some hints and tips on how to keep your cat interested in and stimulated by her toys:

- **Offer your cat** toys that are likely to stimulate known play behaviours (see next page).
- **Make sure** that your cat has a whole range of toys stored away out of sight. Only offer her one or two toys at a time and keep replacing them with different ones.
- **Toys should be a variety** of different shapes and colours.
- **When playing with your cat** do not let her get frustrated. If she looks as if she is becoming confused or frantic, change the game.
- **Be ingenious** when playing with your cat. In the wild, a mouse will try very hard to get away from a cat: it will move quickly and will try to hide. It will not attach a piece of string to its head, throw it over a branch and then dangle itself in front of the cat's nose!

• **Be prepared to experiment** with everyday objects. For instance, some cats are fascinated by the plastic screw-tops off milk containers. The more variety the better.

• **Older cats** rely more and more on their owners to initiate games. Your adult cat will be less likely to want to play on her own.

You can also provide your cat with an adventure playground of some sort to stimulate locomotor play. The following are a few ideas:

• **Cardboard boxes** for your cat to climb in, on and over.

• **Tough paper bags** turned into tunnels by opening them at both ends.

• **Rugs** moved to form tunnels and secret compartments.

• **Cushions** on the floor to hide behind.

• **The ultimate is a climbing frame** – There are many different types available commercially. The largest reach from floor to ceiling and have several platforms incorporating sleeping zones and feeding areas.

A selection of well-known object play behaviours

• **The chase** – A cat runs after a moving object. Toys that you can roll or pull along the floor at speed will stimulate this behaviour. My cat Gorbachov loves chasing nuggets of food that I flick across the room and can even catch nuggets from quite a distance using his front paws like baseball gloves!

• **The pounce** – A cat crouches with her head on the ground and then treads up and down with her back legs before suddenly leaping forward. Your cat may do this to everyday objects such as a leaf on the carpet. Some kittens will do it to apparently invisible objects. Dragging a toy along the ground, then stopping it suddenly before continuing to move it jerkily often stimulates cats to pounce.

• **The bat** – Using either of her front paws, a cat will swipe at a dangling object or poke one that is on the ground. Suitable objects include ping-pong balls; screwed-up pieces of paper and any safe object that can be dangled.

• **The grasp** – A cat will hold an object between her front paws or in her mouth. A cat may grasp an object in her mouth and then release it by shaking her head. This behaviour is called **The toss**.

• **The scoop** – A cat picks up an object with one of her front paws by curving the paw under the object and then grasping it with her claws.

WARNING

Never leave your cat with wool or any other kind of thread that is either free or attached to a toy. Cats have backward-pointing spines on their tongues. Once they have a piece of thread in their mouths it can be very difficult for them to spit it out. Cotton thread with needles still attached are particularly dangerous and are a well-known hazard.

Territory marking and claw sharpening

Your cat will have a natural desire to claw at specially selected objects in her environment in order to keep her claws in good shape and possibly also to mark her territory. You should encourage and train her to use special scratching posts. There are many different types available. Some climbing frames have scratching stations incorporated into their design.

The following are a few hints and tips on choosing scratching posts and encouraging your cat to use them:

- **Offer your cat a choice** of more than one kind of scratching post of different sizes, shapes and textures in order to give her a choice. You will soon discover which type she prefers.
- **You can make your own** scratching posts from natural objects, such as bark-covered logs or by wrapping natural fibre rope around a short piece of fence-post and screwing it in an upright position to a wooden base plate.
- **Avoid** any scratching post that is covered in a material, such as carpet, that she may find elsewhere in your house and that you will be unhappy for her to sink her claws in to.
- **High-level scratching** – Although some cats seem to enjoy scratching low objects or even those lying flat on the floor, you should also give your cat the opportunity to indulge in some high-level scratching. Make sure that at least one of the scratching posts that you offer her is taller than she is long when standing on her back legs with her body and front legs at full stretch.
- **Despite the fact** that you offer your cat a choice of scratching posts, she may still claw other household furnishings. If you catch her clawing at the sofa or the carpet, distract her and carry her to one of her scratching posts. Attaching a toy such as a plastic ball to a scratching post and letting it dangle invitingly from the top is a good way of attracting your cat over.

Bob the Jack Russell: the tale of a tail

Sadly, not all pets recover as well from their amputation traumas as Peggy did, especially when those amputations are carried out by unqualified amateurs. Bob, a six-week-old wire-haired Jack Russell puppy, arrived at Millbrook in November 1996. He was brought in by a vet who had saved his life several days earlier. Two girls had handed Bob to the vet – he was bleeding to death from having his tail amputated by two travellers. The girls claimed they had been walking down the street with their puppy when two men approached, saying that Jack Russells should have their tails docked.

Allegedly, they took Bob behind a caravan and sliced his tail off with a carving knife. The agony Bob suffered must have been horrendous. On close examination, the vet discovered that it had taken two or three slices to cut the tail clean away. RSPCA Inspector Alison MacVicar interviewed the two girls at the vet's, but later found they had provided a false address.

However, Millbrook's deputy manager Sue Walters was amazed at how unaffected by his trauma Bob seemed: 'He was a very tiny puppy when he first came, about five or six weeks old. I took him home with me the first night and found him to be a dear, game little chap. He wasn't the least subdued from his experience and I could only marvel that something so small could be so resilient.' Sue wasn't the only person at Millbrook to be taken with little Bob's character. He soon became a firm favourite among the RSPCA workers and spent most of his days being fussed over in reception.

But behind the love everybody at Millbrook felt for Bob, there was disbelief and anger at the way he had been treated. 'I was really outraged that someone could be callous enough to do what they did,' says Sue; 'you wonder about their mentality, how anyone is capable of inflicting that much pain. It's hard to get your head around it.' Alison MacVicar says it was 'an unbelievable thing to do to a defenceless animal'. Although the girls had given the vet a false address, Alison tirelessly visited every single traveller camp in the area.

Alison didn't believe the girls' story and was keen to press charges. Alison responded furiously and indignantly to Bob's suffering, which she described as 'cutting off a finger or toe without anaesthetic'. But although it was an act of brutality, Alison knew that it was going to be extremely difficult to put together a water-tight prosecution. She continued to trawl all the camps looking for the perpetrators of this horrific act – without luck. There was also the added dilemma of whether or not the RSPCA should hold on to Bob while they attempted to bring a prosecution. Some cases can take a year to come to court, but legally the RSPCA has no alternative but to keep the animal concerned until the completion of court proceedings when, hopefully, the magistrates will exercise their powers and confiscate the animal into the ownership of the RSPCA.

Finally, it was decided that prosecution in Bob's case would be impossible because the men who cut off his tail could not be found. Alison reflected that the case was 'hopeless, and the men who docked the tail have probably moved on now anyway'. Had she caught them, they could have been prosecuted for cruelty under the Protection of Animals Act, 1911.

Bob looked so tiny and sad in his big kennel, and required a lot of attention. Millbrook volunteer Joan Stubblefield talked to animal behaviourist Rebecca Ledger about Bob's special needs. Rebecca believes that 'because a dog's tail is such an important part of how they communicate with other dogs and the world at large, Bob would have to work twice as hard to relate to his fellow canines'. Rebecca and Joan discussed the best ways of trying to socialise Bob, and how they could enrich his kennel with stimulating toys. I suggested he should join a puppy playgroup (see below) where he could learn to interact effectively with other dogs and their owners.

Joan was delighted at Bob's progress at these classes: 'He was wonderful, a real star. After everything that had happened to him he was good with children, adults and other dogs. He played with my old mongrel, ten-year-old Big Max and had another special friend, Lucy the little Cavalier. He adjusted OK to kennel life but obviously preferred to be among people and action, which is why he ended up spending so much time in reception where everything was going on. We all loved him so much.'

It was in Bob's best interests to be rehomed as soon as possible, and in the meantime he kept attending his regular classes so that he would be fit and ready for the family that eventually took him on. But suddenly and inexplicably Bob became ill and wouldn't eat. Staff thought he had a tummy bug, but when he was taken to the vet, it was found that Bob had a chest tumour. A major operation was considered to be his only chance. Despite all the attempts of the RSPCA team, Bob died under the anaesthetic.

Reactions to Bob's death at Millbrook varied from complete disbelief to overwhelming grief. Joan Stubblefield, who had become particularly close to Bob, was shocked to the core: 'He seemed like such a little survivor, I couldn't believe it when I heard the news.' Sue Walters described the reaction from the other members of staff: 'Of course, we were all devastated. We thought he had a simple tummy bug. It came as a terrible shock because he seemed to be getting on so well.'

Joan Stubblefield has the last word on Bob. She says: 'Nobody can forget him: everybody loved him because he had such an endearing personality.'

Puppy playgroups

As Bob was living in kennels at the RSPCA, he was taken to a puppy playgroup to help him learn to interact with other people and dogs, and to obey simple commands. But all puppies, whether they live in kennels or not, can benefit from puppy playgroups: most good vet centres will be able to put you in touch with one.

Puppy playgroups are good for you and your puppy. You will learn a lot about dog behaviour and body language, as well as the first principles of training that you can put into practice at home. A good playgroup will offer you and your puppy a structured course of instruction, and in turn, your puppy will become familiar with the many different kinds of people, animals and objects that he will encounter during his life.

The course content will vary, depending on the instructor, but you should try to establish that it is run by someone with relevant knowledge and experience, who is also a member of a nationally recognised organisation such as the Association of Pet Dog Trainers or the Association of Pet Behaviour Counsellors (see page 126).

Lucky and unlucky: the different fates of two seals

IN THE LATE 1980S A VIRUS EPIDEMIC WIPED OUT THOUSANDS OF SEALS LIVING IN THE NORTH SEA. FOR THOSE – LIKE ME – WHO LOVE THEM, IT WAS A CATASTROPHE. BUT THE DARK CLOUD THAT HUNG OVER OUR SEAL POPULATION AT THAT TIME TURNED OUT TO HAVE A SILVER LINING. DURING THE EPIDEMIC, VETS AND OTHER WILDLIFE RESCUE WORKERS WERE CALLED UPON TO HELP LARGE NUMBERS OF SEALS IN DISTRESS, AND, AS A RESULT, LEARNED HUGE AMOUNTS ABOUT HOW TO TREAT AND CARE FOR THEM. THE KNOWLEDGE THEY GAINED HAS PROVED INVALUABLE EVER SINCE. TODAY, NEARLY A DECADE ON, SEAL RESCUE IS BOTH A WELL-PRACTISED ART AND SCIENCE, WHICH IS JUST AS WELL, AS ALTHOUGH THE VIRUS EPIDEMIC IS OVER, THE SKILLS OF THOSE WHO CARE FOR ILL, INJURED AND ORPHANED SEALS ARE STILL MUCH IN DEMAND.

Grace: too small to fight

RSPCA centres near Britain's coastline are often called on to assist seals in distress. Young pups who have become separated from their mothers or who have just been weaned and are starting to feed themselves are particularly vulnerable. For RSPCA workers, caring for seals can be a year-round activity, as grey seal pups are born throughout the autumn and winter, and common seal pups start arriving in July.

Grace, an injured five-month-old common seal pup, was rescued by Inspector Ian Jackson, who found that Grace had been repeatedly dashed against the rocks in rough weather and, when he reached her, saw that she was completely exhausted. In her weakened state she wasn't difficult to catch, and fortunately put up no resistance – seals have a nasty bite. He pulled a canvas sack over her head – a seal is less likely to be frightened if it can't see – and eased her body into his van for the journey back to RSPCA Great Ayton.

Since Great Ayton is about ten miles from the coast at Saltburn near

Middlesbrough, staff are often called upon to rescue seal pups that have been washed ashore and are either injured or otherwise in danger. In rough weather seal pups can be washed up rivers by strong tides.

At the centre, Ian and manager Maggie Eden carefully fed a tube down into Grace's stomach in order to give her some badly needed fluid – a special cocktail of salts and sugars dissolved in water.

When they weighed Grace they found her to be a mere 13kg (2 stone), half the weight they thought she should have been. It was obvious that Grace needed urgent specialist attention, and arrangements were made to take her to the seal hospital at the Sea Life Centre in Scarborough the next day. Overnight she had to be kept in the small animals unit at Great Ayton. Maggie and Ian tried to make her as comfortable as possible by keeping her in a dark pen with a red heat-lamp and just hoped she would make it through the night. Says Maggie: 'She had no particular fear of humans, but she was just completely stressed out by the whole situation. First, she had been washed up in the rough weather and then moved to a strange place. Poor thing, she looked so bewildered and afraid.' The important thing was to keep her quiet and in a darkened place until she was moved in the morning.

Once at the seal hospital, Grace was put in the care of marine biologist Simon Foster who usually has about eighteen seals on the premises. He is not a vet, but examined Grace, and was sure that, in addition to being exhausted and malnourished, like so many pups she was also suffering from worm infestations – both in her lungs and intestines. She was kept in a seperate pen in the hospital, where she could be given intensive care. He says: 'Grace's biggest problem was that she was incredibly stunted by the lungworm that made it hard for her to breathe properly, and the gutworm that were absorbing all the nutrients she managed to eat. I started off by feeding her special salt and sugar solutions seven times a day, then moved her on to a fish soup made from herrings and the same solution six times a day. Finally, I moved her on to herrings five times a day, but she was too weak to really eat much.'

As well as her feeding routine, Grace received a complex variety of medication. She was checked by a vet and given treatment for both the lungworm and gutworm infestations, and a special vitamin and mineral supplement to help her recover. To ease her breathing she was given a mixture of powders to help dilate her airways. 'She was with us for ten days,' says Simon, 'and although she fought really hard, I could tell that she was too heavily infested and was fighting a losing battle. In the end, it was her body's reaction to the vast numbers of dying worms in her lungs that killed her. Ironically, the effects of the treatment are sometimes more serious than the live infestation itself.' Grace died a few days later.

Because of the breeding patterns of seals, the Sea Life Centre is hectic all year round. Lungworm is a very common ailment suffered by seals brought into rescue centres.

Simon says: 'Lungworm is relatively easy to diagnose in some cases because, when found, infested seals may be coughing up blood and dead worms. Usually grey seals are better able to cope with lungworm than common seals, because they are bigger. Both types of seal need to keep their weight up in order to to hunt efficiently and get the food they need, and seal pups can eat 4 kg (9 lb) of fish a day. At the moment, around half of the common seals we see with lungworm die, but we've never lost a grey seal with the same infection. However, we've been developing a new treatment with a Dutch seal sanctuary, so we hope to have a much better survival rate next year.'

Sick or injured seals are kept at the centre and given medical attention until they recover their strength. When they are better, Simon has to wait until the seas are calm enough to return them to their natural homes. Simon is passionate about his work and clearly adores the seals, but describes them as the 'Father Jacks' of the animal world. 'They're right old miseries,' he says, laughing. 'If you're not careful they can bite off your finger or eat the toe of your welly.' Seals have individual personalities and some are more responsive than others to humans. They can be curious and affectionate, but we should never forget that they are wild animals who need their natural habitat to live happily.

John: a common problem

Another threat to seals is from the fishing industry. They can be caught in fishermen's nets and carried for miles. Because they are mammals and need to breathe air, they can drown from being tangled in nets, which hold them underwater. They are also in danger from the fishermen themselves, many of whom believe that seals are a nuisance and threaten their livelihood.

In the 1950s and 1960s common seals were hunted for their skins, causing a dramatic decline in the seal population. But seal numbers around Britain's coast have increased since the Conservation of Seals Act, brought in in 1970. The public's attitude towards animal-fur clothing and accessories has also changed, so hunting is unlikely to boom again, but with the increasing human demands on fish stocks, coinciding with larger numbers of seals, fishermen have come to see the seals as competition. They claim that as well as eating

John is a common seal: they can be recognised by their all-over spotted coat – grey seals have fewer spots

fish whole, seals will also damage fish inside nets without actually eating them, so that they cannot be sold.

Inspector Ian Jackson insists that the fishermen's view of seals is due not to nastiness, but to a lack of knowledge: 'Not only do they believe that the seals damage their nets, but that they eat all the fish. The argument that perhaps our waters are overfished is not one that the fishing community gives much credence to.'

One seal who faced the threat of hostile fishermen after being carried upstream was a common seal, named John by Inspector Ian Jackson. When the tide goes out, the seals can often be stranded in shallow waters for hours. Ian received a phone call from onlookers at the scene. They could see that John was unable to get back out to sea, and were worried that the fishermen would kill John if the RSPCA did not intervene. A bystander said: 'They'll kill it if they get their hands on it.'

Fortunately the *Pet Rescue* camera crew, the police and the RSPCA were quickly on hand to prevent John being harmed in any way. One seal had already been killed by the fishermen, and John had to be saved before he met a similar fate. One fisherman was quoted as saying: 'This one wouldn't have lasted five minutes, just like the other one.'

Ian waited on the river bank for John, but, because of all the people standing around, the seal was unwilling to come to land. An added problem was the murkiness of the water, which made it difficult to see exactly where John was. With the presence of the police, the RSPCA and concerned members of the public, the fishermen agreed to co-operate with the capture. One of them offered a net, which was strung across the width of the river, and Ian, with the help of Inspector Derek Hall, drove John downstream, but John managed to get through a small gap in the rocks, and evaded the net. The rescue had to be done as quickly as possible, as if John became entangled in the net, he was in danger of drowning.

Ian waded in up to the waist with two fishermen, but John was proving to be a slippery customer. They wallowed around in the shallow water trying to trap John for some time until eventually he was caught in the net. John struggled, but Ian quickly placed his coat over the seal's head to quieten him, and carried him to the van. John was then taken to the Sea Life Centre in Scarborough, and handed over to be cared for by Simon Foster.

Simon found that John had superficial injuries on his face and back, possibly caused by being caught in the nylon netting. The injuries were so minor – just a few scratches – that they healed by themselves, but, like Grace, John was suffering from an infestation of lungworm. Because he was in good condition, John had the strength to fight his illness, and responded well to treatment. Within a few weeks he was able to leave the seal hospital and was able to join the other seals outside in the main pool.

John stayed there for a few months until the sea waters calmed down and he was released at the end of February in Lincolnshire. Simon travelled with John to RAF Donna Nook on the Lincolnshire coast for his release. It was, for Simon, an emotional moment: 'John was released along with another seal from the hospital and we watched them swim out together. The sun was setting and as they reached the wash they were joined by a group of other seals and all swam off together. It was a lovely moment and not one I will forget easily. It makes the job worthwhile to see them returned to their natural habitat, fit and ready to face the rest of their lives.'

All seals that come into the Sea Life Centre are tagged, which helps marine biologists like Simon Foster to monitor their progress. As attached as everybody at the Sea Life Centre had become to John, it was hoped that after

John recovering at the seal hospital in Scarborough

his release he would not be seen again and that he would enjoy a happy, healthy life in the wild where he belongs.

What to do if you see an injured or abandoned seal pup

Leave them alone, do not attempt to touch them or go near them. Seals can be very dangerous, aggressive animals and the best thing you can do is simply to let them be and contact your nearest animal rescue centre, which will arrange for the animal to be rescued by professionals who know what they are doing. Seal pups may look cute, but they have sharp teeth, and will be very frightened of anyone approaching them. So call the nearest animals rescue centre, and observe the seal from a distance until qualified help arrives.

How to recognise seals

There are two types of seal indigenous to the British Isles, the grey and the common seal. It is possible to see both types of seal in a number of places around the coast, most commonly in Scotland. They look quite similar, particularly if you can only see a head coming out of the waves. The ways to tell them apart are the differences in size, head shape and coat colour, although both seals' coats can look very similar when they're moulting.

Adult male grey seals grow to about 2 metres long (6 ft 6 in), and females are about 15 cm (6 in) shorter. Males are much heavier than females. They have elongated muzzles and an irregularly spotted, variable coat.

Common seals have more snub-nosed profiles and are spotted all over. They are much smaller than grey seals, and there is less difference in weight between the male and female.

Sheila Anderson, author of *The Grey Seal* in the Shire Natural History series, says that it's possible to confuse seals with otters, which swim in sea water in coastal areas, although the otter is much smaller. A seal, though, is more likely to turn and look at you, while an otter will disappear as soon as he spots you.

Far from wearing seal-skin products these days, people are much more interested in observing seals in the wild. Seal colonies around Britain's coast can easily be visited by boat, and trips to the Farne Islands in Northumberland, or around the coast of Scotland or Norfolk are very popular with holidaymakers and tourists. But seals are easily disturbed, so rather than taking your own boat out to see them, always go on an organised trip.

Abbey: when the law about dogs is an ass

ABBEY'S STORY IS PROOF THAT A COMPULSORY DOG REGISTRATION SCHEME IN THIS COUNTRY IS WELL OVERDUE. IN MY VIEW, DOG OWNERS SHOULD BE HELD ACCOUNTABLE FOR THE WELFARE OF THEIR ANIMALS. BUT THAT CAN ONLY WORK IN PRACTICE IF ALL DOGS ARE PERMANENTLY IDENTIFIED AND THE DETAILS OF THEIR OWNERS HELD ON A NATIONAL DATABASE. AT THE MOMENT THERE IS NO WAY OF PROVING WHO A DOG'S OWNERS ARE, WHICH WAS THE PROBLEM FACED BY THE RSPCA INSPECTORS DEALING WITH ABBEY'S CASE. IF HER OWNER'S DETAILS COULD HAVE BEEN TRACED, THEN IT WOULD HAVE BEEN POSSIBLE TO PROSECUTE THEM FOR THE APPALLING NEGLECT SHE SUFFERED. AS IT TURNED OUT, THEY BOTH GOT AWAY SCOT FREE AND THERE WAS NOTHING THE RSPCA COULD DO TO PREVENT ONE OF THEM FROM TAKING ABBEY HOME AGAIN.

Prosecuting owners in alleged cruelty cases can be a long-drawn-out and complicated process for the RSPCA. The RSPCA receives a vast number of complaints of animal cruelty a year – 101,751 in 1996 alone – all of which must be investigated. The investigations try to establish the facts. In some cases enough evidence is gathered to mount a prosecution, which can then take months to go through the courts. Last year 971 people were convicted of animal cruelty by the RSPCA.

The story of Abbey the bull mastiff illustrates just how different these cases can be, and how areas of uncertainty can influence the outcome.

In June 1996, Inspector Ken Snook received a call saying that a dog had been left alone while her owner went on holiday. The caller had heard the dog barking for several days before realising that she was unsupervised and alone. Ken arrived, could not get any answer from the house, and looked through the letter box, where he could see Abbey inside.

In keeping with RSPCA guidelines, Ken was not permitted to break into the house and take Abbey away to be cared for in kennels until he had verified over a period of forty-eight hours that Abbey was indeed abandoned. During those two days, Ken put food through the letter box and waited until, accompanied by a keyholder, he could gain access to the house and rescue her. What he found shocked him to the core.

No provisions had been made for Abbey's welfare in the absence of her owner. There was just an open bag of dried food and no water for her to drink. Poor Abbey had been forced to drink from the toilet bowl: by the time Ken got into the house she had drunk the toilet bowl dry.

Ken described the unbelievable squalor he found: 'Abbey was distressed, dehydrated and thin.' Over thirty piles of excrement were found in the house, some of which had turned green. The indications were that Abbey had been left alone for about six days, but the level of mess found inside proved that she had in fact been living indoors for much longer than that. It was impossible to establish the true facts of this case, and, while enquiries were being made, Abbey was emergency-boarded at RSPCA Millbrook in Chobham, Surrey.

Millbrook's deputy manager Sue Walters was furious about the ill treatment Abbey had suffered, and was surprised to find her so friendly: 'She was incredibly trusting and friendly when you consider what she'd been through. A really lovely dog, so affectionate and not in the least aggressive towards humans.'

It took several weeks to track down Abbey's owner. When she was finally found, Mrs X claimed that, although she and her partner were living apart, she had arranged for him to care for the dog while she was on holiday, but said that he had obviously not kept his word. She willingly signed the dog over for rehoming and Abbey stayed at RSPCA Millbrook for about five months while the RSPCA prepared the case for prosecution.

One of Millbrook's animal care assistants, Rick, became great friends with Abbey during her time in kennels, and insists that, despite her past experiences, the dog was far from mistrustful and responded well to people: 'Abbey is a brilliant dog who can get on with everybody: she's rolling over on her back for tickling within minutes.' Rick spent time with Abbey every day and, along with other members of staff at the centre, was looking forward to seeing her go to a caring family once the prosecution was over.

Towards the end of Abbey's fifth month at the centre, Mrs X's estranged partner turned up out of the blue. He claimed that the dog was a gift from his wife, but that, when the couple split up, Abbey had been left with his wife. He said that she had never asked him to look after Abbey while she was away, and had no right to sign her over to the care of the RSPCA.

The situation was more complex as, although Mr X could not prove his ownership of the dog, the RSPCA could not disprove it. Mr X strongly denied he was to blame for Abbey's condition, because at that time he had not been living with Abbey and his wife. He maintained he loved the dog, and, when shown pictures of the squalor Abbey had been found in, he burst into tears.

Mr X fulfils none of the criteria the RSPCA sets for the rehoming of dogs. He works all day and has no garden space for the dog: he lives in a house with a small yard. Although it was felt that Mr X was not able to give Abbey a suitable home, because he said she was his dog there was nothing legally the RSPCA could do to hold on to her. Contrary to the RSPCA's rehoming policy, Abbey left its care without being neutered. Again, because Abbey was already owned by Mr X, the RSPCA had no way of enforcing its neutering policy.

Ken Snook describes how he felt about this case: 'Clearly there were strained domestic circumstances in this case and you'd be surprised just how many cruelty cases are linked to domestic problems. Pets get shoved into the background and are on the receiving end of all the unhappiness.'

Sadly, Mr X came and took Abbey away while Rick was not around to say goodbye to his special friend. Rick has now gone to work with the Army Veterinary Corps and says of her case: 'I was pretty choked that I didn't get to say goodbye to Abbey, but you just have to toughen up.' Ken Snook has been allowed visits to Abbey, who looks fit and content in her new surroundings.

Dogs and the law

Depending on where you live, the precise laws that relate to dog ownership may vary. As a dog owner you will definitely have to obey some national laws and probably other more local ones.

In general, these laws aim to protect the welfare of all dogs and to ensure that dogs are not a public nuisance. Any and all legal responsibilities apply to the person in charge of a dog, and not just the owner. Should an offence be committed, the relevant person may be prosecuted and, if found guilty, penalties such as fines and even imprisonment may apply.

Dog laws in England and Wales

Following are some of the major and most relevant points covered by the laws relating to dogs that are currently in force in England and Wales. In these countries, the responsibility for dogs is split between the Home Office, the Department of the Environment and the Ministry of Agriculture, Fisheries and Food. Details of the dog laws in other parts of the UK vary, and should be checked with the Scottish or Northern Ireland Office.

• When in any public place, all dogs must wear a collar with the name and address of the owner either permanently written on the collar itself or on a disc or other badge attached to it. There are certain exceptions such as guide dogs for the blind and other working dogs while they are working.

• It is an offence to be cruel to a dog in any way. This means harming a dog either physically or mentally and not taking any necessary action to prevent him suffering unnecessarily. Cruelty offences include beating, kicking or terrifying a dog, carrying a dog or transporting him in any way that causes him suffering and failing to seek medical attention when necessary. It does not matter whether the cruelty was intended or not. Ignorance is no excuse.

• It is an offence to use a dog to draw a cart on any public highway.

• It is an offence to abandon a dog, whether temporarily or permanently, without reasonable cause or excuse. This includes letting a dog free to fend for himself as a stray or keeping him shut away without care and attention.

• If a dog worries livestock on agricultural land, the person in charge of the dog at the time may be guilty of an offence. Livestock means cattle, sheep, goats, pigs, horses and poultry.

• The keeper of a dog may be liable for any damage done by that dog.

• It is an offence for anyone to use or allow the use of a guard dog at any premises unless the handler, who is capable of controlling the dog, is present and in control of the dog.

• In certain places, it may be an offence to permit your dog to foul the pavement.

• It may be an offence for a person in charge of a dog to fail to remove any faeces that dog may deposit in specially designated areas, for instance footpaths, grass verges, parks, recreation grounds, beaches or gutters.

• In certain designated areas, it may be an offence for a dog not to be kept on a lead.

• Dog bans may be imposed in certain places and under certain circumstances. For instance, dogs are banned from many beaches between 1 May and 30 September each year.

• In some areas it may be an offence for dogs to be taken into certain public places.

Dog ID

There is currently no mandatory dog registration scheme in the UK (except for those included under the Dangerous Dogs Act) and dogs may be registered in one of a number of voluntary schemes having first been identified in a unique way. The common methods are special collar tags or discs, tattoos and implanted microchips. If you lose your dog, you are much more likely to be reunited with him if you have a precise description of him and details of his vital statistics, and have identified him and registered his and your details on a national computer database.

Despite looking closely at their dogs every day, few owners are able to describe in detail their dog's appearance. If your dog is lost, you will want to tell as many people as possible exactly what he looks like. And if he is found you will need to prove that he is yours before you can take him home. Even though it is not yet a legal responsibility in the UK my advice is that you should identify and register your dog. Both my dog Jessie and my cat Gorbachov are microchipped and registered and that is the method that I would recommend. All dogs and cats adopted from RSPCA rescue centres are automatically microchipped. It's worth noting that microchips can be used to identify almost any kind of animal – from Shire horses to snakes.

The microchip

It would have been much easier to establish Abbey's true owner if she had been microchipped. A microchip is a tiny device that is injected under a dog's skin, usually in his neck. Contrary to what many people think, it does not send out an electronic signal all the time. Rather, it requires another piece of electronic equipment, called a scanner, to 'read' the unique identifying information that is programmed into the microchip. The scanner is only able to pick up the presence of a microchip at short range.

In my experience, implanting a microchip causes no more discomfort than a vaccination injection. It's all over and done with so quickly that most dogs don't even notice that they have been 'chipped'.

Most vet centres, all local authorities, the RSPCA and most other animal rescue organisations have microchip scanners. When a stray dog is brought in it is immediately scanned to see if he or she is microchipped. The scanner beeps when it picks up the presence of a microchip and then displays its unique code. It is then a simple matter of ringing the national register concerned to identify the contact details of the animal's owners.

Having your pet microchipped will cost between £25 and £35. It is a one-off payment and you and your pet will remain on the register concerned for the life of your pet.

No matter how you identify your pet you should still keep your own record of his appearance and vital statistics. Photograph him in good light from a number of angles. Draw a simple body map of him and mark on it the location of any distinguishing marks such as scars or markings that are impossible to see on a photograph. For example, what are the colour of his eyes? The pictures and other details will help you put together an accurate description for circulation to the police and to animal rescue centres should he go missing. You will also be able to use them to create your own fly-sheets and posters.

For more details of identification methods and registration schemes ask at your local vet centre or contact the RSPCA.

How the RSPCA rehomes a pet

The RSPCA's aim is to rehome all healthy unwanted animals that come into its care. Animals are allowed to go to homes in which a healthy and happy lifestyle appropriate to their species can be reasonably assured.

Many potential adopters are visited by the RSPCA to establish whether their homes are suitable (see below), and the Society carries out post-adoption visits as well. If an animal proves to be unsuitable for its owner, the RSPCA requires it to be returned.

It is the Society's policy that all dogs and cats, both male and female, should be neutered, and identified by an implanted microchip (see page 121), as well as identity discs for dogs as part of the rehoming procedure. All animals should also be vaccinated as necessary.

Dogs are never rehomed to be used as guard dogs.

Adopting an animal

The RSPCA has to make sure that animals go to suitable homes. So when you visit a centre and decide to adopt an animal, an RSPCA worker will ask you questions about how your home and family situation will affect your new pet. Potential dog owners, for example, are required to be at home for much of the time, as dogs that are regularly left alone for periods longer than four hours can be disruptive or destructive. The RSPCA will make sure you understand the responsibilities of looking after an animal, such as checking that you know how much your pet is likely to cost you in food, veterinary fees, and so on, and that you have thought about how your pet will be cared for when you go on holiday.

A home-checker will definitely visit your home, partly to make sure that you have enough space, when the animal being rehomed is:
- a large or difficult dog
- an exotic species
- a horse or pony
- a farm animal
- a rabbit.

You will usually have to pay a fee when you adopt an animal, and fees vary depending on which centre you adopt from.

You and the RSPCA

Pet Rescue has introduced thousands of people to the work of the RSPCA, and the programme's appeals have found happy homes for many animals. Some of the appeals – such as the one to find a home for Guy Fawkes, a cat who had been badly burnt after someone threw him on a bonfire – have received between 700 and 800 calls. With this enthusiasm, it's obvious that everyone watching the programme would like to help animals. But it's important to know what you can do to help – in all sorts of situations.

What you can do to stop cruelty to animals

If you see, hear or know of someone being cruel to animals, you can help. The most important thing is to KEEP CALM. If you act immediately, you may be able to stop the person acting cruelly – but think of yourself, and remember that they might turn on you.

If you have a camera or camcorder, take photographs or film what's happening: otherwise, try to remember as many details as you can. Write notes at the time and keep them for reference. Describe people and animals, what the person or people are doing, and what the effect is on the animal.

Telephone the RSPCA's 24-hour cruelty helpline on 0990 555999. You should be ready to give the following information: your name, address and telephone number (these will be treated with the strictest confidence, and will not be divulged without your permission); the name(s) and address(es) of the person or people involved, if you know them; the date, time and place of the offence; the names and addresses of any witnesses; and the registration number and description of any vehicle involved.

You will also need to state whether you would be prepared to testify in court if it became necessary. You will then be asked to give a detailed description of what you saw or heard. Remember, you are providing vital evidence that may be used in a prosecution and memory fades fast!

What you can do to help an injured animal

As you have read in the chapters on Grace and John the seals (pages 109-115), and waterfowl (pages 68-72), unless you really know what you're doing the best thing you can do is to call in the experts. Ring a local vet centre or the RSPCA and ask for their advice: if there is a good local wildlife centre, they may well put you in touch with it.

In the spring, when many wild animals produce young, well-meaning people often 'rescue' fledglings or fox cubs they think have been abandoned, and bring them to the RSPCA. Most of these animals are better off left alone: once they have come into contact with humans they will be less able to survive in the wild.

It's quite normal for fox cubs as young as four weeks old to spend their days alone. If the cub's eyes are open and it looks healthy, leave it alone. If it's on a road, or somewhere exposed or dangerous, move it carefully to a safe place off the road where its mother can find it, but try to handle it as little as possible. If the animal is obviously sick, injured or distressed, call a vet centre or the RSPCA for advice. If it appears injured and you are confident you can handle the animal without causing it further injury or harming yourself, get it to a vet centre or local wildlife centre as soon as possible.

The RSPCA's advice is similar for fledglings. A fledgling is a young bird that has grown all or most of its feathers, and it's quite common for them to leave the nest before they can fly. Its parents are probably nearby, and won't approach until you've moved on. If you are worried, come back in two hours' time – it will probably have gone. If it's in an exposed or dangerous place, move it to somewhere safe nearby where its parents can find it. If you find an unfeathered bird, you could try to find its nest and put it back carefully. If you really feel the bird needs care, contact the RSPCA.

You can read more about foxes in the RSPCA publications 'Orphaned foxes' and 'Foxes in your neighbourhood?', and more about wild birds in the leaflets 'Care of sick, injured and orphaned birds' and 'Feeding wild birds in your garden'.

You can get these and other leaflets by sending an SAE to the Purchase and Supply Department at RSPCA headquarters (address on page 127).

What you can do in the event of an accident

The best course of action is to be prepared: carry the names and telephone numbers of vets in your area with you, and keep a note of the RSPCA's 24-hour telephone helpline. You should also keep a note of your local police station, as any accident involving a dog must always be reported to the police.

The RSPCA publishes a useful leaflet entitled 'First aid for animals'. You can request this leaflet by sending an SAE to the Purchase and Supply Department at RSPCA headquarters (address on page 127).

Your actions matter

There are about sixty million people living in Britain. You may feel that the actions of just one person – you – are a drop in the ocean and that your views will make no difference. But remember that there are thousands - perhaps millions – of others that support the same issues as you, and together we make a difference. Remember that the RSPCA was started by three people who cared about animals: today the RSPCA investigates over 100,000 complaints of alleged cruelty to animals every year, and actively campaigns for improvements in the lives of farm and laboratory animals. The RSPCA makes a difference, and so can you.

Useful contacts

Association of Pet Behaviour Counsellors
PO Box 46, Worcester WR8 9YS. Tel:
01386 751151
email apbc@petbcent.demon.co.uk
A professional body for practising pet
behaviour therapists who work exclusively
on referral from vets.

Association of Pet Dog Trainers
Peacocks Farm, Northchapel, Petworth,
West Sussex GU28 9JB. Tel: 01428 707620
An association primarily concerned with
ensuring fair methods are used when
training pet dogs. It publishes a directory of
pet dog trainers whom it has assessed.

Blue Cross
Shilton Road, Burford, Oxfordshire OX18 4PF.
Tel: 01993 822651
Fax: 01993 823083
A practical animal welfare charity that finds
caring homes for unwanted dogs, cats and
horses and provides veterinary treatment for
animals whose owners cannot afford
private vet fees.

British Goat Society
34-36 Fore Street, Bovey Tracey, Newton
Abbot, Devon TQ13 9AD
Tel: 01626 833168
This organisation aims to safeguard goats
against cruelty and to improve the various
breeds of goat. It is also committed to
increasing the supply and consumption of
goats' milk.

British House Rabbit Association
PO Box 346, Newcastle-upon-Tyne, NE99
1FA
Helpline: Anne Mitchell (Southern Counties
Area Co-ordinator) 01403 267658
Provides education on looking after rabbits,
and information on behaviour problems and
breeds. It is building a database of vets who
specialise in rabbit care and is campaigning
to ban the sale of rabbits in pet shops.

British Small Animals Veterinary Association
Kingsley House, Church Lane, Shurdington,
Cheltenham, Glos GL51 5TQ
Tel: 01242 862994
A professional body for those in small
animal practice, teaching and research.

British Veterinary Assocation
7 Mansfield Street, London
W1M 0AT. Tel: 0171 636 6541
A voluntary professional body
representing veterinary surgeons.

Commissioner for Consumer Policy (Mme
Christiane Scrivener)
Commission of the European Communities,
200 Rue de la Loi,1049 Brussels

Environment Agency
Tel: 0800 807060 (emergency hotline),
01645 333111 (general enquiry line)
Protects and enhances the whole
environment.

Guide Dogs for the Blind
Hillfields, Burghfield Common, Reading,
Berks RG7 3YG. Tel: 0118 983 5555
Provides and trains guide dogs, and
teaches the blind in their use.

Hearing Dogs for the Deaf
The Training Centre, London Road,
Lewknor, Oxon OX9 5RY.
Tel: 01844 353898,
Fax: 01844 353099
A registered charity and non-membership
body that trains dogs to respond to
household sounds by touching their deaf
owners and leading them to the source of
the sound.

Irish Society for the Prevention of Cruelty to
Animals
300 Lower Rathmines Road, Dublin 6,
Republic of Ireland.
Tel: 00 353 1 497 7874
A registered charity that aims to prevent
cruelty to animals and to promote kindness
in their treatment.

Ministry of Agriculture, Fisheries and Food
(MAFF)
MAFF Helpline, Room 11, MAFF Whitehall
Place, West Block, London SW1A 2HH.
Helpline: 0645 335577
Calls charged at local rate. The helpline
provides official advice on importing pets and
animals, exporting plants, vegetables, fruit,
fruit trees, soil, peat etc., food labelling, and
information on the ministry's publications.

National Canine Defence League
17 Wakley Street, London EC1V 7LT. Tel:
0171 837 0006
A registered charity devoted to protecting
and defending all dogs from abuse, cruelty,
abandonment and any form of mistreatment
in both the UK and abroad.

NGRC Retired Greyhound Trust
149A Central Road, Worcester Park, Surrey
KT4 8DT. Tel: 0181 335 3016
Launched in 1974 (registered as a charity in
1975), the organisation was set up to relieve
the distress and suffering of ex-racing
greyhounds, and to find good homes for
them.

People's Dispensary for Sick Animals
PDSA House, Whitechapel Way, Priorslee,
Telford, Shropshire TF2 9PQ
Britain's largest veterinary charity. It
provides free treatment for sick and injured
pets of owners who cannot afford the
payments themselves.

Pets as Therapy
6 New Road, Ditton, Kent ME20 6AD
Tel: 01732 872222
Has 10,000 members across the UK who
take their pet dogs into hospitals. All dogs are
assessed for their suitability and provided
with an identity disc.

Proteus Reptile Rescue and Sanctuary
204 Slade Road, Erdington, Birmingham
B23 7RJ.
Tel: 0121 384 6033
Fax: 0121 382 9176
A voluntary organisation specialising in
reptiles.

Rare Breeds Survival Trust
National Agricultural Centre, Stoneleigh
Park, Warwicks. CV8 2LG.
Tel: 01203 696551
A national registered charity established for
and dedicated to the protection of
endangered breeds of farm animals.

Royal College of Veterinary Surgeons
62-64 Horseferry Road, London SW1P 2AF.
Tel: 0171 222 2001
The UK statutory body for the veterinary
profession. Its role is principally to maintain
standards of professional conduct and to
ensure that education for veterinary
surgeons is of the highest level.

Royal Society for the Prevention of Cruelty
to Animals (RSPCA) Headquarters
Causeway, Horsham, West Sussex RH12
1HG.
Tel: 01403 264181(general enquiries)
Cruelty hotline: 0990 555999

Scottish Society for the Prevention of
Cruelty to Animals
Braehead Mains, 603 Queensferry Road,
Edinburgh EH4 6EA.
Tel: 0131 339 0222
A registered charity that aims to prevent
cruelty to animals and to promote kindness
in their treatment.

Ulster Society for the Prevention of Cruelty
to Animals
Unit 4, Boucher Business Centre, Apollo
Road, Belfast BT12 4HP.
Helpline: 0990 134329
A sister organisation to the RSPCA, this is a
registered charity that aims to prevent
cruelty to animals and to promote kindness
in their treatment.

Wood Green Animal Shelter
Kings Bush Farm, London Road,
Godmanchester, Cambridgeshire PE18 8LJ.
Tel: 01480 830014
Fax: 01480 830566
Established in 1924, this charity is primarily
involved with animal rescue and providing
homes for unwanted or abandoned pets.

World Parrot Trust
Glanmor House, Hayle, Cornwall TR27 4HY.
Tel: 01736 753365
Registered charity committed to raising
money for conservation projects, and
involved with international parrot causes.

Acknowledgements

The publishing of any book is a team effort, and I would like to express my sincere thanks to the many organisations and to the individuals – human and other animals – who have played a part in creating this book.

I am particularly indebted to the following: those who contributed to the front cover, especially Molly the horse, Sue Walters and Dusk, Joan Stubblefield and Max; RSPCA staff, in particular Justine Pannett, Pippa Bush and everyone at Millbrook and Great Ayton; Deborah Bosley; Kate Quarry; Peter Heathcote of Proteus Reptile Rescue; David Poole of the NGRC RGT; Susan Knowles of the British Goat Society; Interpet for providing information on Mikki Dog Training Discs; the National Canine Defence League; Jerry Young; Phil Healey; all the people who adopted the animals featured in this book – and of course all my friends and colleagues who work on *Pet Rescue*.

The publisher would also like to thank the Kennel Club Library, Julia Barnes, author of *The Complete Book of Greyhounds*, and Andrew De Prisco and James B. Johnson, authors of the Reader's Digest *Book of Dogs*, for information on greyhounds.